MW01118619

This book and others in the series
have been prepared to give you a
better understanding of a chronic illness.
Armed with the latest information
on all aspects of ASTHMA,
you will be able to minimize the problems
and substantially improve the
quality of life.

Understanding
and
Managing
ASTHMA

EDITORS

JOHN L. DECKER, M.D.
AND
MICHAEL A. KALINER, M.D.
THE NATIONAL INSTITUTES OF HEALTH

Other Avon Books in
THE RELIABLE HEALTHCARE COMPANIONS Series

UNDERSTANDING AND MANAGING ARTHRITIS
UNDERSTANDING AND MANAGING DIABETES
UNDERSTANDING AND MANAGING HYPERTENSION
UNDERSTANDING AND MANAGING OSTEOPOROSIS

Coming Soon

UNDERSTANDING AND MANAGING ULCERS

Avon Books are available at special quantity discounts for bulk purchases for sales promotions, premiums, fund raising or educational use. Special books, or book excerpts, can also be created to fit specific needs.

For details write or telephone the office of the Director of Special Markets, Avon Books, Dept. FP, 105 Madison Avenue, New York, New York 10016, 212-481-5653.

THE RELIABLE
HEALTHCARE COMPANIONS

Understanding
and
Managing
ASTHMA

EDITORS

JOHN L. DECKER, M.D.

AND

MICHAEL A. KALINER, M.D.

THE NATIONAL INSTITUTES OF HEALTH

AVON BOOKS ◆ NEW YORK

The editors would like to thank Hugh Howard, John Gallagher, and Paul Cirincione, whose writing and research assistance helped make this series possible.

THE RELIABLE HEALTHCARE COMPANIONS: UNDERSTANDING AND MANAGING ASTHMA is an original publication of Avon Books. This work has never before appeared in book form.

The medical and health procedures contained in this book are based on research recommendations of responsible medical sources. But because each person is unique, the author and publisher *urge the reader to check with his physician before implementing any of them.*

The author and publisher disclaim responsibility for any adverse effects or consequences resulting from the suggestions or the use of any of the preparations or procedures contained herein. No one should ever commence taking drugs or discontinue a prescribed drug regimen without first consulting a physician.

AVON BOOKS
A division of
The Hearst Corporation
105 Madison Avenue
New York, New York 10016

Copyright © 1988 by Gallagher/Howard Associates, Inc.
Published by arrangement with Gallagher/Howard Associates, Inc.
Library of Congress Catalog Card Number: 88-91545
ISBN: 0-380-75427-4

All rights reserved, which includes the right to reproduce this book or portions thereof in any form whatsoever except as provided by the U.S. Copyright Law. For information address Avon Books.

First Avon Books Trade Printing: October 1988

AVON TRADEMARK REG. U.S. PAT. OFF. AND IN OTHER COUNTRIES, MARCA REGISTRADA, HECHO EN U.S.A.

Printed in the U.S.A.

OPM 10 9 8 7 6 5 4 3 2 1

To our teachers and patients alike
this book is dedicated. So often
the two are one and the same.

Table
of
Contents

A NOTE TO THE READER

There was a time when the physician prescribed in Latin and was likely to respond to a patient's questions with knowing paternalism. ("Now, don't you worry about a thing. That's my job.") Today, healthcare providers—doctors, nurses, and therapists—are beginning to accept the notion that the better informed the patient is, the more likely it is that the patient's condition will improve. There has been, in fact, a clear movement in recent years to harness the patient's curiosity about his or her ailment and put it to use in understanding its nature and treatment. But both patient and doctor face new challenges as a result.

Those doctors who are inclined to educate their patients find themselves so steeped in science and loaded with facts that their explanations often fluctuate between oversimplification and information overload. And those patients who want to be educated have to overcome the comforting notion that the infallible doctor can fix everything. We live in a world where the patient is offered unrealistic hopes of easy cures and instant pain relief by television advertising and media enthusiasm. We have come to believe that there is a harmless pill for every problem and that cures are the norm rather than the exception. While medical science has made incredible progress in understanding the structure and function of living things, there are still innumerable unanswered questions. Sometimes patient and doctor must face these questions together.

The fact is that, despite the pulsing excitement of research advances, we are practicing today what Dr. Lewis Thomas has called "a halfway technology." We are in a state of mildly confused uncertainty as to what is the preferable choice of action in many medical circumstances. It is this uncertainty, this clangor of divergent advice from many specialties, to which THE RELIABLE HEALTHCARE COMPANIONS series addresses itself, in the hope that it can enable patients to participate intelligently in decisions about their own medical care.

This book and the others in the series are meant to lead you in your quest for more knowledge, more help, and more support. Your illness may be confusing, and especially in the case of asthma, its underlying causes likely to be obscure. But we should all understand as much as possible about what is happening to our bodies. By using the resources identified here in conjunction with the guidance offered by your healthcare providers, you should develop a solid foundation for a counterattack at your ailment. I wish you success.

John L. Decker, M.D.
Director, Warren Grant Magnuson Clinical Center
THE NATIONAL INSTITUTES OF HEALTH

PREFACE

The problem for most people who are confronting a personal health problem like asthma is knowing where to begin.

This healthcare sourcebook differs from the other books on the market in that it is a catalogue of help designed to tell you what to expect of your ailment. Further, this book will enable you to find the kinds of help you need in treating—and learning to live with—your asthma, or your child's asthma.

Every patient is a unique traveler through the medical landscape. There are no two patients who have the same manifestations, the same course, and the same qualitative and quantitative constellation of accompanying problems. But just as the same map can be given to and used by many travelers, so a sourcebook of help can be relevant to many asthma sufferers as they begin their patient education. You know best your unique problems and concerns; you do not have the same need for information, treatment, and support that your doctor's other patients do; your lifestyle will require unique adjustments that only you can know and make.

But whatever your specific needs, in this book you will find:

- An authoritative yet accessible and comprehensive overview of the problem of asthma, including answers to your questions regarding physical and emotional management, medications, and special problems confronting children with asthma;
- Key information about the role of specialists, community healthcare agencies, and consumer support groups;
- Detailed advice on confronting and dealing with the day-to-day concerns of adjusting to the treatment of asthma through the use of various devices that dispense medication;
- A detailed evaluation of the best available books and other publications about asthma;
- A separate and detailed evaluation of audiovisual materials available for rent or purchase;
- Specific advice on how to get access to these kinds of help (including 800 toll-free numbers, addresses, and names.)

Increasingly, the medical profession has come to acknowledge the value of patient education. Particularly with a chronic illness like asthma, you as an educated patient can, with the cooperation of your doctor, use medication and other therapies and strategies to help control your ailment and make it more manageable.

Take advantage of the help in these pages, and of the innumerable sources of help out there to understand asthma: you don't have to fight it alone, nor should you leave it alone.

Understanding and Managing
ASTHMA

INTRODUCTION

Asthma, which derives from the Greek word for panting, or breathlessness, is a serious disease that can be life-threatening. However, while it's largely incurable, it is a reversible and treatable disease. With effective management by a trained doctor and a thorough program of patient education, which includes the informed support of friends and family, most asthma patients can and do learn to live normal lives.

In economic terms, the impact of asthma is devastating. The annual cost of hospitalization due to asthma attacks is in excess of $2 billion, with more than 400,000 hospital admissions. The cost of over-the-counter products for the treatment of asthma in 1986 alone was $2.3 billion.

Asthma affects adults and children. From 4 to 7 percent of all preadolescent children in this country are sufferers, with boys outnumbering girls two to one. Some estimates project that one in fifteen children will have at least one asthma episode, and one in forty will have repeated episodes before the age of seventeen.

Asthma is a disease that is frequently misunderstood by the public—and often poorly treated by doctors. Although we are learning more about what causes it, we don't always know why asthma occurs the way it does. Since many doctors are not properly trained to treat this very complicated disease, the asthma patient is well advised to seek a specialist for the treatment of his or her asthma problems.

The Breathing Process

When you breath in, your chest expands. The expansion creates a negative pressure, allowing air to move freely and deeply into the airways and down into the lungs. The air you breathe in is rich in oxygen, which is vital for all the body's functions. The lungs take up the oxygen to deliver it to the rest of the body, and replace it with carbon dioxide. When you exhale, the chest contracts, the airways within relax and become smaller, and the spent air, which is rich in carbon dioxide, is driven out.

During breathing, the chest cavity opens up in all directions. Asthmatic problems begin when an airway is narrowed, whether it's due to a muscle spasm, swelling, inflammation, or mucus buildup. Although a partial obstruction of the passageway will occur, breathing will open up the airway (because of the expansion, the airway grows larger while the obstruction remains the same size). Air will move normally into the lungs.

When it comes time to breathe out, the elastic lung collapses in all directions. That's normal. However, the obstruction then becomes relatively larger and acts like a one-way valve: you can breathe in, but breathing out becomes more difficult, and the exchange of good for bad air becomes inefficient.

Not all the air we breathe in is exchanged on every breath. A healthy person's lungs and airways can hold about 5 liters of air (a liter is close to a quart), but he or she will exchange only about 3 or 3.5 liters in a deep breath. As a result, more than a liter of air remains untouched in the lung. But in the asthma sufferer, the obstruction in the airways will trap more and more air in the lungs.

The lungs of a typical asthma patient can also hold about 5 liters of air. Unfortunately, the asthma patient might have two or three times as much air trapped in the lungs as the normal person. Thus, the asthma sufferer is able to take in considerably less oxygen. In addition, the lesser amount of oxygen is diluted with the trapped air, resulting in a mix that is rich in carbon dioxide and poor in oxygen.

The presence of the trapped air means that even when relaxing, the asthmatic is keeping the lungs partially full—which explains why it is so tiring for him or her to breathe. When the asthma becomes severe, the patient may be unable to get air in or out because there is no available space left. This is a life-threatening situation some people with asthma face.

If you have never had an asthmatic episode, take a partial breath and hold it. Keeping that volume of air within, try breathing on top of it. That roughly approximates the sensation of breathing for the asthmatic.

What causes these obstructions to occur in asthma patients will be discussed in detail in Chapter 1. For now, however, we are going to examine those parts of our anatomy that play important roles in the breathing process.

The Lower Respiratory Tract

To understand what happens during asthma attacks, we must first understand normal breathing, a process we call ventilation. It involves two systems, the lower and upper respiratory tracts. The lower respiratory system includes the lungs, bronchial tubes, and alveoli; the upper respiratory tract includes the mouth, nose, and sinuses.

LUNGS: We all are born with two of them, one located on each side of the chest. They are surrounded by a chest wall made up of ribs and muscles plus the diaphragm, the thin muscle that separates the chest cavity from the abdomen or stomach cavity. When the size of the chest cavity increases, it forces the lungs to expand and to take in air. The chest actually empties by relaxing, as the lungs, like filled balloons, push the air out thanks to their elastic properties.

BRONCHIAL TUBES AND THE ALVEOLI: Air is carried into and out of the lungs by a system of air ducts that looks very much like an upside-down tree. The air is drawn through the nose or mouth and down into the throat via a large trunk or windpipe called the trachea. When the trachea reaches the lungs, it divides into two main branches called bronchial tubes. In the lungs, the bronchial tubes divide into thousands of other branches (bronchioles) which get smaller and smaller.

At the end of each branch are the alveoli, or the leaves of our tree. These are tiny, delicate balloonlike air sacs lined with very small blood vessels covered in a very thin membrane. It is at this point that the air in the lungs and the blood flowing through the lungs make their exchange. The blood takes on the fuel of fresh oxygen and drops off the waste product of carbon dioxide.

The respiratory system not only looks like a tree, but it acts a little like one, too. A tree feeds itself by reaching down to its roots to absorb water and minerals from the soil, while it also reaches for sunlight and carbon dioxide through its branches and leaves. The lungs do something similar to feed themselves. The lungs are nourished by sugars, fats, proteins, and minerals from our foods, which are absorbed by the intestines (the equivalent of roots for the purposes of our analogy). In the alveoli (the leaves) an important exchange takes place. There, the red blood cells that flow through the blood vessels that line the walls of the alveoli pick up the oxygen in these air sacs and give up the carbon dioxide.

The tree analogy actually extends to real trees, too. The waste product of our respiratory system, carbon dioxide, nourishes trees (and all plant life), while the waste product of plants, oxygen, is necessary for our nourishment.

The Upper Respiratory Tract

Although asthma occurs because of obstructions in the airways of the lungs, which are part of the lower respiratory system, the upper respiratory tract should not be overlooked in the discussion of asthma.

MOUTH: The mouth is one of the two air channels to the lungs and, therefore, can be the point of entry for substances that can cause asthma symptoms. However, in normal breathing, the air goes through the nose, and only when the nose can't provide an adequate air exchange does the mouth take over.

NOSE: The nose is a double-barreled airway. Inside, there are three coiled bones, called turbinates, which are attached to the side walls of each airway. The biggest ones, the inferior turbinates, fill a good part of the lower half of the nose on both sides, while the middle turbinates fill much of the upper half. The superior turbinates are tiny projections form the roof of the nose.

The lining of the nose contains tiny bristles called cilia that trap particles found in the air we breathe. As a result, air is filtered as it passes through the nose. The airways in the lungs are also lined with these sweeping bristles. To help trap irritants on the cilia, cells lining the airways of the nose are covered with a moist and sticky mucus. When irritants are caught in the mucus, the cilia move them to the front or back of the nose, where the impurities are either blown from the nose or swallowed.

SINUSES: Along each side and at the back of the nose are four sets of cavities called sinuses. These empty spaces act as resonators for the voice. When they are inflamed or filled with fluid, the resonance of the voice is lost.

The sinuses are connected to the airways by short openings, called ostia. As with the airways of the nose, the sides of the sinuses are covered with mucus and lined with tiny cilia. The mucus in the nose and sinuses is made in mucous glands and in specialized cells called goblet cells. Among its other functions, the mucus moistens and warms the incoming air so it is closer to our body temperature. The mucus on the surface of the larger airways in the lungs also acts to filter, moisten, or warm (or, in some instances, cool) the air. If the upper respiratory system becomes infected so it can't do its job, the lower respiratory system acts as a backup and takes over part of the filtering, warming, and moistening tasks.

INFECTIONS OF THE NOSE AND SINUS: The upper and lower respiratory systems not only work together, but they occasionally grow sick together. As they are lined with the same tissue that secretes mucus, it's possible for viruses or bacteria to infect the nose, sinuses, and airways. Consequently, when an infection develops in the nose or sinuses, people with asthma should take precautions that the lower respiratory system also doesn't become infected, a condition that could lead easily to an asthma attack. (See discussion of sinusitis, page 26.)

The upper respiratory system can also affect the lower respiratory system if polyps develop. Polyps are small, pale growths in the lining of the nose and sinuses that block the openings (ostia) of the sinuses in the nose, preventing the normal drainage of mucus or pus from the sinuses. When this occurs, the mucus fills the sinuses and an infection can result, which can provoke an asthma attack. When polyps are removed, people with asthma may experience some relief from asthma attacks brought on by the polyps.

CHAPTER 1

The Disease

Myths and Misunderstandings

Asthma is such a common ailment that most of us know an asthmatic. Because we've heard about the problem for years, we may well have a sense that we understand it.

Ironically, this very familiarity with asthma is quite likely to have given us a false—or at least an incomplete—understanding of the ailment. In order to lay the framework for a more complete picture of asthma and its sufferers, let's look at some of the common misconceptions.

MYTH: "Asthma Is Psychosomatic." Many people have the impression that asthma is caused by emotional disturbances or can be brought on, almost voluntarily, by emotional stress. Consequently, asthma is often thought to be psychosomatic, or "all in the head."

This notion is wrong; worse yet, it tends to make the disease seem less important than it is. It places a great deal of guilt on the patient with asthma and even on the parents of a child with asthma. Parents may come to believe that somehow they are responsible for the disease.

The fact is, asthma is a physical disease. Even if some of the biochemical changes that occur during psychic stress can lead to a triggering of asthma symptoms, that does not indicate that asthma is caused by emotions.

MYTH: "Asthma Is Contagious." Only infectious diseases are contagious, and asthma is not among them. While you may inherit a tendency to develop asthma from your family, it does not follow that you will inevitably develop allergies other members of your family have—or, for that matter, their asthma.

7

If family members have asthma, that doesn't mean that allergies are the cause of their asthma symptoms. It can be said that someone is at greater risk of developing asthma or allergies, or both, if the disease exists in their family, but it just isn't assured.

MYTH: "Asthma Can't Be Cured." Some people with asthma, especially children, seem to outgrow or recover from their asthma, never to experience a flare-up again. This is not the norm, however, as most people with asthma experience symptoms periodically throughout their lives.

On the other hand, the good news is that asthma, by definition, is reversible. The damage it causes is not permanent, as is the case with a lung disease like emphysema. Asthma is a manageable disease, and with proper treatment, the asthma sufferer should experience fewer and less severe symptoms.

MYTH: "People With Asthma Should Not Exercise." Although exercise can trigger asthma symptoms in some asthmatics, it doesn't in many asthma sufferers. And even in those for whom exercise is a clear trigger (children in particular), the asthmatic episodes can often be effectively prevented with medications and exercise regimens.

We will talk at length later about exercise and asthma, but, in brief, swimming is thought to be a better exercise than jogging because the air near the surface of the water is moist and warm, which decreases the likelihood of an asthma attack being induced. But whatever the form of preferred exercise, most people, with the help of their doctor, can learn to exercise moderately without asthma symptoms.

MYTH: "Children Outgrow Their Asthma." It is true that about half the children who develop asthma between the ages of two and eight have a dramatic reduction in symptoms in their teenage years; unfortunately, it is also true that many of them experience asthmatic episodes later in life. As a result, it is dangerous for parents to elect not to treat asthma because they believe their child will outgrow it over time.

This is a serious mistake on several grounds, including the fact that many children develop asthma at the same time as their self-image is forming. The untreated child, consequently, can go through life thinking of himself or herself as physically impaired. Restricted exercise patterns may also result in a significant real loss of muscular development.

In short, you can't afford to presume your child will "outgrow" an asthmatic problem.

MYTH: "Asthma Leads To Emphysema." Asthma does not cause emphysema, a crippling lung disease. Asthma affects only the airways, whereas emphysema is a disease that damages the air sacs, or alveoli, permanently impairing the exchange of oxygen and carbon dioxide in the blood. Emphysema is irreversible, whereas asthma can be reversed.

MYTH: "If You Didn't Have Asthma As A Child, You Won't Get It As An Adult." The onset of asthma can occur at any age, although it is true that children are more likely than adults to develop allergies and asthma for the first time. However, if you suspect that you have asthma for the first time and you're over fifty, see your physician, as the problem may be related to your heart.

MYTH: "Wheezing Is A Sure Sign Of Asthma." Although wheezing is perhaps asthma's most distinctive mark, all that wheezes is not asthma. Some people who wheeze, often almost imperceptibly, do so because of an obstruction in the throat, not in the chest.

The wheezing caused by asthma is a distinctive rattling, squeaky noise that sounds almost like a buzz inside the chest. In mild attacks of asthma, the wheezing can be so faint that many patients take little notice.

During a moderate or more severe attack, the bronchial airways may be partially blocked, causing a wheeze in the chest. The wheezing is usually much louder and longer upon exhalation, but in severe attacks it will occur even when breathing in. It is a sign that air is having trouble getting out.

The absence of wheezing doesn't necessarily indicate the absence of asthma. If the airways are only slightly obstructed, the patient may experience a tightness in the chest rather than a wheeze. Coughing is an occasional sign of asthma, too. In life-threatening conditions, the blockage of the airways is complete and there are no wheezes to be heard, as no air is moving through the airways whatsoever.

MYTH: "Asthma Is Always Due To Allergies." Allergies and asthma are often brethren, but each exists without the other in many cases. With hay fever, for example, it is thought that about 30 percent of patients develop asthma; on the other hand, a majority of people with allergies do not have asthma. Furthermore, a family history of allergy does not mean that an asthma patient is to be diagnosed automatically as having allergic asthma, although it is certainly more likely than not to be the case.

MYTH: "You Can't Die Of Asthma." Asthma-related deaths do occur—as many as 40,000 people may have died from the complications of asthma in the past ten years. When asthma becomes a life-threatening problem, one or more of the following factors plays a role:

- The asthma is of long duration and has gone largely untreated;
- The asthma medications have been misused or ignored;
- The asthma attacks are sudden and severe.

MYTH: "A Change Of Climate Will Help The Asthmatic." This is true . . . but only sometimes. Patients whose asthma is brought on by allergies can move to areas where the offending allergen is not present. Similarly, for patients whose asthma is caused by infections, a move to a warm, dry climate may provide benefit. However, in most cases, a change in geography does not provide the long-term help hoped for by the patient.

A major goal of proper treatment of asthma caused by allergies is, of course, the removal of the offending allergen. But since most cases of asthma are complicated by several—or even many—allergens, irritants, and weather changes, a major relocation to escape one or a few allergens may not significantly reduce the symptoms. Other, less expensive strategies are usually recommended, such as air-conditioning units or home air-filtration devices.

What Happens During an Attack

All asthma episodes involve an "attack" on the airways of the lungs. Episodes may focus on the large air passages (bronchi) or the smaller passages (bronchioles), but all make breathing difficult.

The trachea, the first part of the respiratory tract, usually is not involved in asthma, so when an infection develops in the trachea, it seldom brings on an attack. The trachea is larger than the other airways and more rigid because it is wrapped in cartilage, a dense connective tissue. The bronchi, which are smaller than the trachea (but larger than the bronchioles), also have supporting cartilage.

The disease of asthma is found primarily in the smaller airways because they are more easily obstructed. Not only are the bronchioles smaller, but because they have no cartilage, excess mucus, swelling, and inflammation can block them more easily.

Asthma attacks vary in severity. In almost 4,000 cases a year, people die from them. In some of these instances, the patients' respiratory tracts produce so much mucus that they literally drown from it. At the opposite end of the spectrum, a blockage of the bronchioles may produce only a mild attack, one that is almost indiscernible, recognizable only after the patient takes a breathing test. (See page 42.)

Attacks also vary in duration. Some last only a few minutes, whereas others may last hours or even days. They can come on gradually or suddenly. Depending on the severity of the stimulus, an asthmatic can go from being perfectly healthy to being very sick in a matter of minutes.

How Asthma Blocks Air in the Lungs

Whether the focus of the attack is on the large or small airways, one, two, or all of the following conditions will exist:

- The bronchi and bronchioles in the lungs are squeezed tight by the action of the muscles surrounding these airways;
- The mucus secreted by the cells in the lining of the respiratory tract plugs the airways;
- A swelling in the walls of the airways narrows the air channels.

The invariable result is that the individual with asthma is unable to breathe normally because air cannot pass freely through the airways.

MUSCLE TIGHTENING: Wrapped around the outside of the air tubes, including both bronchi and bronchioles, are muscles that, by tightening and relaxing, may affect the size of the tubes. In people without asthma, the muscles around the airways are relaxed. While everyone's airways have the potential for closing in response to irritants such as air pollutants and cigarette smoke, the asthma patient is especially sensitive to airway irritation. Simple allergens such as cat hairs or ragweed can cause the muscles to tighten dramatically, an event known as bronchospasm, producing difficulty in breathing.

Besides irritants of many sorts, an asthma patient with allergies may experience asthma episodes brought on by weather changes, infections, exercise, and emotional stress. In effect, hundreds of substances or conditions can cause the bronchial muscle to tighten the airways.

INFLAMMATION: Asthma attacks can also be caused by inflammation of the lining of the airways.

Inflammation is a defense mechanism by which the body reacts protectively against an invasion of its tissues. Heat and redness result when the body dispatches additional blood to the affected region to protect itself. Among the other blood products delivered to the site of inflammation is a virtual invasion of white blood cells. One type of white blood cell is called an eosinophil, and it is the presence of this one cell type that characterizes an attack of asthma. In fact, diagnoses of asthma are made, in part, by looking for this cell.

The white blood cells are there to protect against whatever has caused the airways to become inflamed. The white blood cells come in and attack the bacteria or virus and often are themselves killed in the process, an event that triggers the release of substances called enzymes that are intended to kill the foreign invader. Unfortunately, in the case of asthma, the dying white blood cells cause problems. The buildup of dead cells causes more swelling and irritates the lining of the airways, further increasing the inflammation.

MUCUS: A third mechanism by which airflow obstruction occurs is excess mucus secretion. During an asthma attack, the mucus which normally serves to aid safe and comfortable breathing increases to the point that it clogs the airways. In normal circumstances, the airways can be cleared by coughing up the mucus, but during an asthmatic episode there is so much mucus, and the passage is so swollen, that the airways cannot be cleared.

The mucus, which is released from the mucous glands and goblet cells lining the respiratory tract, is necessary to lubricate the airways and protect them from damage. It also is armed with specific substances that are designed to kill viruses and bacteria. Again, in the case of asthma, when the body produces more mucus than is necessary, it becomes a problem rather than a solution. Ironically, in the asthmatic the excess mucus and white blood cell production that are responses to what the body sees as dangers to its health become in themselves health threats.

Differences in Episodes

As we discussed earlier, asthma episodes can range from extremely mild to life-threatening. The seriousness of an event depends on the health and age of the person as well as his or her history with the disease. Asthmatic episodes can be restricted to a specific time of year or occur throughout the year, although some asthma patients are never free of symptoms.

The status of one's asthma is not fixed, so someone with mild asthma may develop a more severe form. On the other hand, with proper treatment a case once thought to be severe may become so successfully managed that it could be called "mild." In light of all these variables, the following categories are meant to provide a general overview of the differences that exist between episodes of asthma. Note also that the three categories of "mild," "severe," and "life-threatening" refer not only to the seriousness of the symptoms but to their frequency as well.

MILD ASTHMA: Mild bouts of asthma may be distinguished from more serious varieties in that they interfere with the sufferer's quality of life, but they almost never interfere with sleep, work, or school. They usually do not require frequent visits to the doctor.

In a mild attack, the airflow may become sufficiently restricted that when the patient expels a breath, he or she produces a wheezing or whistling sound. The asthmatic with a mild case may also develop a cough, find it difficult to clear mucus or phlegm from the lungs, or experiences a slight tightness or heavy feeling in the chest.

For some, a mild attack of asthma is a "twitching" sensation of the lungs. It can be brought on by seemingly innocent activities such as exercise or a burst of laughter. However, since a person with asthma has an inherent sensitivity to airway irritants, the possibilities for producing asthma symptoms are numerous and varied (see page 17). They range from better known substances such as dust and pollen to cold air and fear. Hayrides, cigarette ashes in an ashtray, or cat hair on someone's coat can pose a threat. Attacks can occur during the day or at night, and they may come without warning or develop gradually.

Most mild episodes subside in a few minutes with medication. Medication may be used not only to treat symptoms, but also to prevent symptoms from occurring, especially in the case of asthma induced by exercise, exposure to cold air, or exposure to irritants and allergens known to the patient. Sometimes all that is required is a brief rest to bring relief.

SEVERE ASTHMA: People with more severe asthma experience fairly regular bouts of asthma symptoms. (This type of asthma is frequently referred to as "perennial asthma.") Most people with perennial asthma have moderate to severe symptoms on most days of the week. They may feel as if they are literally fighting for their breath, or they may develop a long and debilitating cough. If the episode is severe, the ensuing panic over the struggle for air may further contribute to the asthma attack and actually prolong it, making it all the more difficult to recover.

Severe attacks differ from milder episodes in that the breathing is more difficult and the duration of the attack longer. A severe attack can make the asthma patient short of breath, even when the patient is sitting still. It can become worse when the patient lies down, does any exercise, or even talks. The wheezing usually is much louder and longer upon exhalation, but in severe attacks it will occur even when breathing in. It's usually loud enough to be heard by others. In the most severe attacks, it can be a great struggle just to get enough used air out of the chest to make room for the next shallow breath of fresh air.

Patients with severe asthma describe their struggle for air in terms of trying to draw their breath through a straw. Others have characterized their experience as "a gasping search for air," "drowning," and "feeling like they were being buried alive."

LIFE-THREATENING: Most asthma episodes are not life-threatening, but in some individuals asthma has been known to cause a fatal attack. The most serious type of episode, called status asthmaticus, occurs when the breathing difficulties cannot be corrected with the usual medications and the resulting lack of oxygen becomes critical. Also termed "continuous severe asthma," status asthmaticus can persist for more than twenty-four hours, in spite of oral, inhaled, or injected medications.

It is important to note that many cases of status asthmaticus can be avoided if patients are alert to recognize any early airway problems and seek early treatment.

AFTER THE ATTACK: Between episodes, many asthma patients show no discernible signs of having the disease. They don't experience any symptoms whatsoever, and there is no wheezing or coughing to suggest that they have asthma. Even tests designed to determine the condition of an asthmatic, such as a breathing test called a spirometry (see page 42), will not necessarily show any signs of asthma during these intervals. Often after a sudden attack of coughing and wheezing that lasted a full hour, people report that they have only some muscle soreness in the chest.

This is not the case with everyone. Unfortunately, many people with long-term asthma are never free of their asthma symptoms. Some experience a constant tightness or "twitchy" feeling in their chest or even a steady cough when they breathe deeply; others seem never to be able to shake a persistent wheeze when breathing in or out.

Factors That Can Trigger Asthma Attacks

Asthma is not caused by any single known organism or toxic substance. However, it is known that hereditary factors and allergic reactions play a significant role in many, if not most, cases.

Different factors produce asthma symptoms in different people. In some cases, it is the pollen in the air that produces an allergic response, while in others it's a viral infection, an exposure to an irritant like household ammonia, or a change in the weather. At the most basic level, it is the combination of an inherent disposition and the exposure to an environmental factor that produces the asthmatic event.

The Two General Types of Asthma

There are two general categories of asthma—allergic asthma and nonallergic asthma. The principal difference between the two types is the nature of the factor or factors that trigger the asthma symptoms.

ALLERGIC ASTHMA: A person with an allergy has an unusual sensitivity to substances known as allergens that have little or no effect on most people. These substances may be inhaled, injected, rubbed on the skin, or swallowed. House dust, foods, pollens, animal hair, molds, medicines, cosmetics, and insect venoms are among the more common allergens. The symptoms they produce may be mild, as in a stuffy nose or itchy eyes, or more severe, as in the obstruction of the airways in the lungs.

Allergies are an important cause of asthma flareups in those people who have allergic asthma. About 90 percent of asthma sufferers under age thirty have allergies, whereas less than half of the asthma sufferers over forty years of age have allergies.

Allergic asthma attacks may be related to very specific allergens such as seasonal pollens. At one time, doctors believed that seasonal asthma of this type was caused by only one or a few allergens and that an asthma management program in which patients avoided specific environmental substances would keep them free of symptoms. For most asthmatics, however, such a narrow approach does not work.

Characteristic indicators of allergic asthma are as follows:

- Asthma attacks that are triggered by common allergens such as animal hair, house dust, molds, and pollen.
- Asthma attacks that occur upon exposure to seasonal allergens (for example, asthma that occurs only in the spring or fall in response to grass or ragweed pollens).
- A family history of allergy, eczema (an itchy reddish skin inflammation), or runny nose (rhinitis).
- Positive skin tests for specific allergens (see page 44).

NONALLERGIC ASTHMA: About one in three people with asthma do not have allergies. The attacks experienced by those with nonallergic asthma are not the result of contact with known allergens but are triggered by upper respiratory tract infections, bronchitis, influenza-type illnesses, aspirin or related compounds, sulfiting agents used as preservatives, irritants encountered in the workplace, or other irritants.

Children frequently experience their first asthma symptoms as a result of viral bronchiolitis, a respiratory infection that usually occurs only in children less than two years old. Sometimes the infection develops into a persistent cough or croup, and about 50 percent of these children develop a recurring wheeze. The good news is that this kind of asthma is usually mild in nature and is usually controlled or in remission by the age of eight.

Some adults with nonallergic asthma have no signs of asthma at all—except when they develop an infection. Such persons usually remember having had a viral infection when they were younger which led to a period of chronic and sometimes severe nonallergic asthma.

Characteristic of nonallergic asthmatics are the following:

• Negative skin tests for specific allergens (see page 44).
• The absence of any family history of allergy or ezcema.

Factors That Can Trigger Asthma Symptoms

The following factors are known to play a role in inducing asthma symptoms.

ALLERGENS: Allergens are substances that cause allergic reactions when susceptible people eat or breathe them, have them injected, or have them come into contact with their skin. Not everyone who has allergies has asthma, and not everyone with asthma has allergies. However, for people inherently disposed to asthma, allergic reactions frequently lead to asthma symptoms.

There are two categories of environmental allergens that cause allergic reactions: outdoor and indoor allergens. Outdoor allergens are usually pollens from plants or spores from molds, fungi, moss, and ferns that are carried in the air. The most important sources of indoor allergens, which are found primarily in the home and the workplace, are house dust, cockroaches, mites, animals, feathers, mold spores, smoke, and plant pollens.

The time at which the asthma symptoms occur can offer a clue as to the offending substance. In the spring, seasonal pollens from grass and trees are often the problem, whereas in the fall it probably is ragweed. Unfortunately, animal hair, house dust, and molds are examples of allergens that can be a problem year-round. If you suffer from asthma symptoms twelve months of the year, you should examine the possibility that house dust plays a major role in those symptoms.

House Dust: House dust is not made up of any one substance but is a varied mixture of potentially allergenic (allergy-causing) materials. It may contain fibers from different types of fabrics, including wool or cotton lint, bacteria, mold and fungus spores (especially in damp areas), food particles, human or animal flakes of skin or hair, bits of plants and insects, and other allergens peculiar to an individual home. Other important components of house dust may be disintegrated stuffing materials from pillows, mattresses, toys, and furniture, as well as disintegrated fibers from draperies, furniture coverings, blankets, and carpets. The breakdown of these latter materials from use and age seems to enhance their ability to sensitize susceptible persons.

Mites: The ability of house dust to trigger asthma symptoms is also related to mites, which are microscopic spiderlike insects. The house dust mite generally proliferates in the summer, when there is a minimum humidity of 65 percent and usually a temperature of at least 70 degrees. As a result, denizens of high altitude areas like Denver and very dry areas like Phoenix have few problems with these allergens.

When the house dust mite that proliferated in the summer dies—as it does with seasonal temperature and humidity changes—its body disintegrates into fragments that reach the respiratory tract easily and account for some of the wintertime allergies. The house dust mite also excretes little fecal balls which fall to the floor and get buried in carpeting. When the house is closed up in the winter, the mite balls are brought up into the recirculated air whenever someone walks on the carpeting. Although the mites are dead, their disintegrated bodies and fecal matter continue to pose threats as winter allergens.

Molds: Molds can be a part of house dust, but they can also be a separate problem that appears at different times of the year.

Of the thousands of different fungi, all of them fall into two categories: yeasts and molds. Yeasts are thought to be more allergenic than molds, but molds are stressed here as they are commonly found in house dust and can cause allergic responses. What makes them so troublesome is that the spores of the molds are so small that they evade the protective mechanisms of the nose and upper respiratory tract to reach the lungs and bring on an allergic asthma attack. Like pollen, molds are an important cause of seasonal hay fever. People who are allergic to molds may have symptoms from spring to late fall. However, unlike pollen, molds may persist after the first frost and can grow in the house year-round.

Pollen: Pollens are well-known allergens, but not all pollens are allergenic. It's the chemical makeup of pollen that is the basic factor that determines whether a particular type is likely to cause hay fever. The types of pollen that most commonly cause allergic reactions are produced by the plain-looking plants (trees, grasses, and weeds) that do not have showy flowers. The most allergenic pollen comes from plants that produce it in high quantities—a single ragweed plant, for example, can generate a million grains of pollen a day. In addition to ragweed, sagebrush, redroot pigweed, lamb's quarters, Russian thistle (tumbleweed), and English plantain are prolific producers of allergenic pollen in the United States.

Animals: Another major source of allergens is animals, particularly cats and dogs. Animal hairs or dander (flakes of skin or hair) are often implicated as the cause of allergies, although the allergen is actually the saliva from both cats and dogs. Cats provide a more potent source of allergens because they preen almost constantly, covering their coats with salivary proteins which then become airborne with lost fur.

In general, dogs that don't slobber are less allergenic than those that do, but broad generalizations can be misleading. For example, someone who is sensitive to one kind of animal or cat isn't necessarily allergic to all other similar animals or cats. In more than a few cases, patients have learned that they are highly sensitive only to a specific breed of cat or dog.

Cockroaches: These ancient insects are also a potent source of allergens, particularly in urban environments. The cockroach is a newly appreciated allergen, but it's clearly a significant problem in urban areas where cockroaches are commonplace. Some people have tested negative to everything except cockroach allergens. The specific source of an allergen is the dried parts of the cockroach body. The only strategy for this allergen is cockroach control.

IRRITANTS: Irritants can cause asthma symptoms but, again, only in people who have asthma or are susceptible to the disease.

The air we breathe on the job is considered a significant cause of asthma for many people. Some studies report that up to 15 percent of all cases of asthma that arises in adult men are caused by irritants in the workplace. People with asthma should be concerned if airway irritation occurs on the job, especially early in the work week. The tightness in the chest that you might be inclined to dismiss as tension could be the beginning of an airway obstruction.

It is not just bad air on the job that poses a threat to many people with asthma. Modern life generates pollutants that linger in the air for days and weeks, generally in and around cities, which may damage the lungs by irritating the airways.

Certain pollutants increase airway reactivity even in normal people. Examples of some common irritants that are a particular problem for people with asthma are:

- cigarette smoke
- perfumes
- strong odors
- newsprint
- cold air
- rapid changes in the weather

INFECTIONS: Infections can cause the lining of the bronchial tubes to swell, reducing the size of the air passages and making breathing difficult. Two important causes of infections are viruses and bacteria.

Viral Infections: It is widely believed that respiratory viruses play a more significant role in the production of asthma than bacterial infections. It is not understood why, but simple viral colds seem to settle more quickly in the chest and develop into a wheeze or cough for the person with asthma. Compounding the problem of viral infections is the fact that antibiotics are not effective in the treatment of viral infections.

Bacterial Infections: The case for respiratory bacterial infections seems to be different. At one time it was believed that these infections were a serious cause of asthma, but that is no longer thought to be the case. Bacterial infections certainly can lead to an asthma attack (asthma symptoms can develop following bronchitis or pneumonia), but more often it is thought that the bacterial infection is a result of the asthma attack and occurs because the excess mucus that collects in the bronchial tubes becomes infected when it can't be cleared.

Obviously, this does not mean that bacterial infections should be ignored. On the contrary, for someone with asthma, any kind of a bacterial infection of the sinuses (see "Sinusitis," page 26) or viral infection increases the risk of an asthma flareup. Even a simple congestion of the nose, sinuses, or throat can lead to an irritation of the lower airways of the lungs. As a result, you should treat all colds carefully in order to reduce the chances of more serious complications. If the mucus from the nose or chest becomes yellowish or greenish in color, you can be assured that an infection is present and should be treated immediately. Unlike viral infections, bacterial infections can be treated effectively with antibiotics.

EXERCISE: "Exercise-induced" asthma usually follows moderate to strenuous exercise. It is not unusual for the asthma symptoms that follow exercise to be mild and to disappear spontaneously after a period of rest. In any case, they usually disappear with proper treatment.

Most people with allergic asthma will have symptoms of wheezing during or following exercise. The symptoms are not solely restricted to wheezing, but can include an accelerated heart rate, coughing, and chest tightness five to ten minutes after exercise.

Asthma symptoms are not thought to be triggered by the strain placed on the airways by exercising. Rather, it is the way we breathe during exercise that causes asthma to develop. The air flowing over the moist mucus actually causes the water to evaporate, creating a heat loss. Thus, the airways are cooled and, it is thought, this cooling and drying irritates the airway and causes the asthmatic episode to occur.

A patient need not exercise to reproduce exercise-induced asthma. By breathing rapidly, in fact, one can take in enough cold, dry air to produce asthmatic symptoms. As a result, it is believed that it is not the strain of the exercise but the air taken in during the exercise that produces symptoms in those who are prone to exercise-induced asthma. Furthermore, the presence of air pollutants, such as sulfur dioxide, high pollen counts, and viral respiratory tract infections, also increases the severity of wheezing following exercise.

As we saw earlier, a common misconception, especially among parents, is that asthma sufferers should not exercise at all for fear of an asthma attack. To avoid exercise for these reasons is in most cases neither necessary nor wise. Only in rare instances is it necessary for the person with asthma to avoid moderate exercise.

Proper exercise will help maintain better overall health and body function. If the patient is overweight, exercise will help him or her lose weight, which helps the lungs because they won't have to work as hard. If the exercise is dynamic and places a moderate strain on the heart, which is the objective of aerobic exercise, it will, over time, increase the patient's ability to carry out daily activities without undue fatigue and to respond to sudden physical and emotional stress without an excessive increase in heart rate and blood pressure.

Today, with proper detection and treatment with specific drugs, exercise-induced asthma can be effectively controlled and even prevented. (See "Medication," page 46.)

The best form of exercise for those who experience exercise-induced asthma is swimming or activities that require only brief intervals of exercise. Swimming is highly recommended because the air at the surface of the water is especially warm and humid. Something of the same effect can be achieved by jogging with a face mask.

EMOTIONAL FACTORS: Emotions can indirectly contribute to asthma symptoms. However, this does not mean that asthma is psychosomatic or that it is emotional in origin. Instead of asthma being "all in the head," which it certainly is not, it could be said more properly to be "all in the chest."

Stress can cause or aggravate the disease, as we saw earlier, although often the patient must first have an underlying disposition for the disease. It would be incorrect and unfair, then, to characterize asthmatics as people who have emotional problems. That may be true in some cases, but it certainly wasn't the emotions that brought on the asthma: in all likelihood, it was the other way around. It is important to understand that emotions play a role in many areas of our personal health—both in contracting certain diseases and recovering from them. But the person with asthma must not be made to feel that he or she is responsible in any way for the disease, especially if he or she is easily distressed.

FOODS: A food allergy is a hypersensitivity to certain foods. As with the other allergens, exposure to the offending food—that is, the consumption of it—produces symptoms that range from an upset stomach or a stuffy nose to a remarkable skin rash. If you have asthma, a simple food intolerance can develop into a full-blown respiratory problem.

There are no foods to which all, or even most asthmatics, are allergic. However, some foods are more suspect than others, especially those that contain mold or sulfites. (See opposite page for a list of common foods containing these substances.) Food containing monosodium glutamate (MSG) may also be a problem in some asthma sufferers.

Chemicals known as sulfiting agents, or sulfites, are commonly added to foods to prevent browning or to act as bleaching agents. Sulfiting agents may also be added to food which does not contain sufficient quantities of vitamin B1. In this instance, the food label will not indicate the presence of the sulfite.

Sulfite sensitivity should be suspected in people with asthma whose symptoms develop or worsen after eating processed or restaurant foods or drinking wine and beer. Even certain medications commonly used in the treatment of asthma contain sulfites. If you suspect that you may be sulfite-sensitive, try to avoid sulfite-containing foods. Alert your doctor, too, as the use of the medications isoproterenol and racepinephrine generates sulfur dioxide, which can exacerbate asthma symptoms for people who are sulfite-sensitive. (See "Medication," page 46.)

MOLD-CONTAINING FOODS

- Beer and wine
- Baked goods containing yeast, such as sourdough and pumpernickel breads
- Buttermilk (this includes sour cream)
- Cheeses that are not processed
- Cider
- Dried fruits
- Mushrooms
- Sauerkraut
- Smoked meats and fish (this includes hot dogs, sausages, and corned beef)
- Vinegar and foods that contain vinegar

FOODS CONTAINING SULFITES
(in order of highest concentration)

- Vegetables served in some salad bars
- Lemon juice
- Dried fruits
- Wine
- Molasses
- Grape juice
- Wine vinegar
- Instant potatoes
- Fresh shrimp

For the adult with long-term asthma, it is thought that food allergies can also act as a trigger. If you suspect that you are allergic to any food, it is recommended that you avoid the food if it is not nutritionally necessary to your diet. In addition, you should be tested for the allergy by an allergist (see page 91). Finally, as an asthmatic you should not eat the foods to which you are allergic under any circumstances: the only prevention for food allergies is avoidance.

Many people confuse food allergies with food intolerances. In general, the symptoms of a food intolerance will be confined to gastrointestinal distress. The key distinction, then, is that an intolerance to certain foods will not create an obstruction of the airways.

(A thorough discussion of food allergies would require a separate volume, for it is a complicated and important subject. For more information, look for those publications discussed in Chapter 5 that deal with allergies in greater detail, and food allergies in particular. Our concern in this book is restricted to an understanding of those food allergies that could trigger asthma symptoms.)

ASPIRIN AND OTHER DRUGS: Even though the exact mechanism has not been determined, some asthma sufferers are intolerant to aspirin. Thus, it is recommended that people with asthma avoid the use of aspirin, as nearly 10 percent of all asthma patients who have used aspirin report that their breathing became more difficult after taking it. Be sure to read labels carefully because aspirin appears in many products, including most over-the-counter preparations designed to relieve pain.

In addition to aspirin and aspirin products, people with asthma should avoid nonsteroidal antiinflammatory drugs, which, like aspirin, are used to reduce pain and inflammation. These medicines, often referred to as "aspirin substitutes," include drugs sold under the brand names Advil, Anaprox, Butazolidin, Clinoril, Feldene, Indocin, Meclomen, Motrin, Nalfron, Naprosyn, Nuprin, Rufen, and Tolectin. If you have asthma, or are known to have aspirin-induced asthmatic episodes, do not take them, since these medications can cause the same asthmatic symptoms as aspirin. Drugs like acetaminophen (Tylenol is one brand of this drug) are rarely the cause of asthma, so if you are aspirin sensitive you may be able to take these products safely.

Asthma patients with nasal polyps and sinusitis, in particular, are discouraged from taking aspirin because the combination of asthma, aspirin sensitivity, and nose polyps can precipitate an asthma attack.

Note also that tartrazine, which is the yellow dye #5 used in a number of foods such as cake mixes and soft drinks, is a rare cause of asthma symptoms in patients who are also allergic to aspirin.

People who must take aspirin (such as certain arthritis patients) but who are sensitive to the drug can have their aspirin sensitivity measured. It is also possible to desensitize them by beginning them on minute doses of aspirin and slowly raising the dose. Eventually they will be able to take normal amounts of aspirin safely. In such cases, consult with your doctor regarding the testing and desensitization processes.

Conditions That Can Trigger Asthma Attacks

We have discussed many of the external factors that cause asthma or play some role in inducing an asthma attack, such as pollens, infections, exercise, and foods. But in this section we are concerned with certain conditions (such as pregnancy) or diseases that can also trigger asthmatic attacks or make asthma symptoms worse.

GASTROESOPHAGEAL REFLUX: Gastroesophageal reflux (GER) is a condition in which some of the ingested food and digestive juices in the stomach flows back (refluxes) into the esophagus, the feeding tube that leads from the mouth to the stomach. It can lead to a disorder called esophagitis and is frequently experienced as "heartburn" (which, despite its name, has nothing to do with the heart). This problem is not uncommon: as many as 45 to 65 percent of adults with asthma and perhaps as many as 60 percent of all children with long-term asthma are believed to have GER. GER and esophagitis are also very common in persons with hiatal hernia, a condition in which part of the stomach pushes through the diaphragm muscle that separates the chest and abdomen.

Irritation of the airways from food and digestive juices brought up from the stomach can trigger asthma in patients with GER. If you have a tendency to belch up acidic stomach contents, a history of heartburn, or frequent nighttime asthma episodes, discuss the problem with your doctor.

Treatment: Many asthma attacks occur at night. It may be no coincidence that reflux of stomach contents is also most likely to occur at night, because when we lie in bed it is easier for liquid materials to pass from the stomach up to the esophagus. If you have difficulty controlling your asthma and you experience reflux, try to do the following:

• In general, eat smaller meals; in particular, schedule the last meal of the day for several hours in advance of bedtime. Don't lie down after eating.

- Do not eat meals that contain highly acidic or spicy foods. Limit or avoid alcohol, as it can add to the acid content of your stomach.
- If necessary, take antacids shortly before going to bed at night.
- Sleep on two pillows or elevate the head of the bed.

PREGNANCY: It is not clear as to why or how pregnancy affects asthma, but statistics indicate that the asthma symptoms of one-third of all pregnant asthma patients worsen during pregnancy. This is particularly true if the mother-to-be has severe asthma or if she gains a great deal of weight during her pregnancy.

Treatment: Although the pregnant asthma patient may be treated a little differently, it is generally accepted that asthma does not significantly endanger the mother or the fetus. However, all medications should be given at their minimal effective dose and frequency, and those not specifically required discontinued. Certain drugs should be avoided altogether in pregnancy, including barbiturates (and barbiturate-containing combination tablets such as Tedral), hydroxyzine, potassium iodide, decongestants such as phenylpropanolamine and phenylephrine, epinephrine, tetracycline, sulfonamides, trimethoprim, and codeine. (See "Medication," page 46.)

In general, inhaling a drug rather than taking it orally will reduce its possible side effects and thereby reduce risks to the fetus. Acute attacks of asthma, therefore, may be managed with inhaled adrenergic bronchodilators or injectable terbutaline. Drugs thought to be safe for use during pregnancy include theophylline, aminophylline, ephedrine, cromoglycate, and properly administered corticosteroids (taken by mouth or inhaled). Medications that are used regularly throughout the pregnancy are the only drugs that should be used during labor. Allergy desensitization therapy (shots) can be continued during a pregnancy.

In cases of first pregnancies, it is advisable that the mother-to-be have her asthma treated by a doctor who is familiar with her history. During pregnancy, she needs to feel confident that she and her baby are quite safe.

SINUSITIS: In the Introduction we talked about the upper respiratory tract and how the inflamed sinuses can present problems for the asthmatic. Specifically, the asthma patient must be concerned with a condition called sinusitis, an inflammation of the lining of the sinuses.

Although the causes of sinusitis are too numerous to be listed here, it is the combination of allergic and infectious sinusitis that has long been considered the most difficult form of sinus disease to treat. Nasal allergies involve congestion, swelling, excess mucus, and sinus discomfort. Infectious sinusitis can be caused by a virus or bacteria. Sinusitis caused by both viral and bacterial infections has been closely tied to asthma attacks. In fact, one study indicated that nearly 50 percent of patients with asthma have had bacterial infections of the sinuses. Whenever mucus is yellow or green, it usually indicates the presence of an infection.

Inflamed sinuses, however, can result from a variety of causes other than an infection. For example, the lining can become inflamed and swollen because of nasal polyps, allergies, or abuse of nasal sprays. Drugs, too, can set off a nasal reaction with accompanying sinusitis. For example, intolerance to aspirin is common in patients with bronchial asthma, nasal polyps, and sinusitis.

Sinusitis may be present even in the absence of a runny or congested nose or fever. The only evidence of sinusitis might be a slight sinus headache. Yet such a case of sinusitis can pose the same risk of an asthma flareup as the more familiar runny nose with green mucus. If there are signs of sinus problems along with persistent asthma symptoms, your doctor may order an X ray of the sinuses. If he or she finds that the walls of the sinuses are thicker than normal, chances are good that the diagnosis will be sinusitis.

Treatment: For mild sinus congestion, the traditional method of inhaling steam through the nose to free the passages is still recommended. Applying a hot water bottle, hot wet compresses, or an electric heating pad to the inflamed area may also offer relief. Drinking clear fluids may help, too.

While these procedures will ease the discomfort of the inflammation, they will not cure it. If the sinuses are inflamed and painful, a nonaspirin preparation, such as Tylenol, may be called for. Again, aspirin is suspect because, in many cases, it can trigger an asthmatic episode.

Decongestants such as Sudafed can be helpful, but antihistamines must be taken cautiously because they tend to dry the lining of the sinuses, which may not help in treating the problem. A topical nasal decongestant, such as Neo-Synephrine, should be used only with a doctor's approval. In addition, nose drops and sprays should not be used for more than a few days, and only with your doctor's supervision, since a not-infrequent side effect of these drugs is more congestion.

Depending upon the suspected cause of the sinusitis, your doctor may prescribe an antibiotic. If you are not allergic, the preferred choice for treating sinusitis is penicillin (or some form of it). Otherwise, the doctor may use an antibiotic such as Tetracycline or Bactrim. Many doctors also use topical nasal steroids to reduce inflammation in the nose and to promote drainage from the sinuses.

In cases of severe sinusitis, your doctor might try one of several other approaches. In one technique, the patient lies on his back with his head over the edge of the examination table. A decongestant fluid is placed in the nose, and air is suctioned out of the nose so that the decongestant fluid can shrink the sinus membranes sufficiently to permit proper drainage to resume. Sometimes a thin tube is inserted into the sinuses to wash out trapped pus and mucus.

It is important that asthma patients not ignore any signs of a sinus problem. Statistics show that patients who have their sinus symptoms treated promptly report fewer asthma flareups

HYPERTHYROIDISM: Hyperthyroidism is a condition characterized by the overproduction of thyroid hormone. One of the most common early symptoms is an unexplained weight loss, despite increased hunger and food consumption. Again, the mechanism that causes hyperthyroidism to exaggerate asthma symptoms is not well known, but if your doctor has diagnosed you as having hyperthyroidism, discuss with him or her the impact it has on your asthma and its treatment.

Health Problems
That Look
Like Asthma

A number of quite different medical problems can look like asthma at first glance. Sometimes they so resemble asthma in the early stages that the correct diagnosis requires a number of visits to your doctor.

The diagnosis should, of course, be left to your doctor; so if asthma-like symptoms persist, don't "self-treat" yourself. Symptoms that suggest defective ventilation, such as wheezing or chronic coughing, are sufficiently important to diagnose properly and treat promptly, especially if there is any history of asthma in the family. If you are not confident of the diagnosis, consult your doctor again.

The following are some of the potential medical problems that can be confused with asthma.

CHRONIC BRONCHITIS: Chronic bronchitis and asthma affect the airways in many of the same ways. They produce some of the same symptoms, such as coughing, excess mucus, and shortness of breath.

Usually the patient with chronic bronchitis has a history of cigarette smoking, and the coughing begins in the early morning hours. When the chronic bronchitis cough persists for years, which it can, it eventually affects airflow much as asthma does.

The diagnosis of chronic bronchitis is usually made by careful evaluation of the patient's medical history with special attention paid to any pattern of smoking. A spirometry exam (page 42) will determine if there is an airway obstruction; a chest X ray may also be done, but for someone with chronic bronchitis it usually will appear normal. In cases of chronic bronchitis, cigarette smoking must be immediately discontinued or the damage will progress and the complications become grave.

EMPHYSEMA: Emphysema differs from asthma in that it attacks the alveolus, or air sac, and the damage it causes is permanent. A patient with emphysema does not cough as much as someone with chronic bronchitis or asthma. The condition's major symptom is shortness of breath, especially during exertion.

Emphysema will only get worse over time. People suffering from the disease breathe abnormally quickly in order to get enough oxygen into their blood. Once again, cigarette smoking seems to play a role in the history of many people who have emphysema. Among nonsmokers, exposure to certain environmental agents and/or a congenital (inherent) condition called alpha-1-antitrypsin deficiency frequently explains the presence of emphysema.

As with asthma, a spirometry will show airway obstruction. Unlike asthma, emphysema often fails to respond to most medications. For example, the airways of the patient with emphysema will show little, if any, improvement after the use of bronchodilators. Even short-term use of steroids may fail to help.

PULMONARY EMBOLISM: A pulmonary embolism, or blood clot in the lungs ("pulmonary" means lung, "embolus" means plug), is not often confused with asthma, but on occasion cells in the clot will release chemicals that cause the airways to narrow.

A correct diagnosis in these circumstances can be difficult. The diagnosis usually involves a specialized medical test in which a chemical "dye" is injected into the pulmonary artery while an X-ray movie tracks the dye flowing along the artery. Any blockage will be obvious on the X ray.

OBSTRUCTION: Wheezing in infants, which may look like asthma, is often due to a foreign object that has been swallowed and become stuck in the throat. Often the wheezing comes from the neck rather than the chest. If you suspect the wheezing is caused by an obstruction, see a doctor immediately. In adults, such wheezing commonly results from a polyp (growth) on the vocal chord, an enlarged thyroid, or even trapped food. In such a case, an otolaryngologist should be consulted for a careful examination of the throat.

CARDIAC ASTHMA: Cardiac asthma is not a kind of asthma at all, but, like the other health problems we've mentioned, it masquerades as asthma.

Cardiac asthma is a term used to describe asthmalike symptoms due to a condition called "heart failure." This is not the same as a heart attack, in that it isn't a sudden failure of the heart to pump. Rather, the heart fails to pump blood effectively. When the heart failure is not properly managed, fluid will collect in the lungs, causing the patient to wheeze. The doctor who suspects heart failure will look for an enlarged heart and liver, swelling of the ankles (more fluid retention), and maybe a swelling of the veins in the neck. With proper medication, people suffering from this malady live normal lives.

THE SECOND OPINION

There are many other medical conditions that are apt to be confused with asthma. The ones we have discussed are only the most common. However, if you suspect that asthma is not the cause of your problem and that it is another illness, or if you have any question about the diagnosis or treatment, it's always recommended that you seek a second opinion.

No longer is the patient who asks for another opinion thought to be a difficult patient. No longer should the patient assume that a good doctor is going to be insulted if he or she wants advice from another doctor. On the contrary, if your doctor objects or tries to discourage you from receiving a second opinion, change doctors. A good doctor wants a confident and informed patient.

CHAPTER 2

Care and Treatment

In the last chapter we discussed what happens to the body when asthma strikes and some of the principal conditions or substances that trigger asthma attacks. The subject of this chapter is what is known today about caring for the person with asthma—adult or child—and what possible treatments are available.

You need a doctor to make the initial diagnosis of the asthma; depending on the diagnosis, he or she will also help you create a self-management program that is designed to deal with the disease and its unique effects on your life. Every effective asthma management program is made up of two essential parts: proper medication and an appropriate program of patient education.

Asthma is a lifelong illness. Although some children outgrow it, most sufferers must learn to live with it. While you may expect to control the disease with proper medication and a prudent program that recognizes and avoids many of the danger areas that can induce attacks, you cannot expect that the asthma will ever go away. However, if the treatment program is successful, the symptoms should occur less often and with less severity.

Therefore, it is critical that you develop confidence in your doctor and his or her program. A proper understanding of your asthma and its treatment will reduce not only your anxiety about the disease but also some of the fear that can fuel asthma attacks.

Consulting Your Doctor

There may be no single treatment decision more important than your choice of a doctor. If the patient is your child, the choice may be doubly important since the doctor must not only treat your child's symptoms but your own understandable anxieties over the child's health. Furthermore, treatment can be adversely affected if a child suspects that his

31

or her parents have any reservations about the quality of medical care the doctor is providing.

For these and other reasons, it is imperative that the patient (and, in the case of children, the parents) feel confident and comfortable in his or her relationship with the doctor regarding all phases of care.

QUALIFICATIONS: Our experience at the National Institutes of Health has been that the doctors who trained in general practice, whether as internists or family practitioners, often have insufficient training in the treatment of asthma and allergies. Doctors trained as pediatricians on average seem more nearly up to the task of treating allergies (after all, allergies are a very common problem among children). Nonetheless, we still recommend that everyone with asthma, even mild asthma, seek the guidance of a specialist.

The fact is, the family practitioner is responsible for hundreds of different diseases; the specialist is interested in—and more knowledgeable about—a narrower range of ailments. In our view, then, when asthma or allergies are involved, the family practitioner should always work with a consultant or the patient should be treated by a specialist.

SPECIALISTS: Nobody is better at diagnosing and treating allergies than an allergist; because nearly 90 percent of all children with asthma have allergies, it is only logical they are best treated by an allergist. On the other hand, only about 50 percent of adults with asthma have allergies, so they have the choice of an allergist or a pulmonologist (chest specialist), unless troubling allergies are involved. Yet here, too, many pulmonologists are inadequately trained in allergies, whereas allergists have had good training in chest medicine; so an allergist is, once again, the best choice for treating the asthma patient. (For further discussion of specialists, see page 90.)

The allergist to choose is one who is board certified, which means he or she has completed training in a program that is qualified to train allergists and has also passed a certifying examination. This exam is prepared by the American Board of Allergy and Immunology, a joint board of the American Board of Internal Medicine and the American Board of Pediatrics. As a result, any board-certified allergist is, in addition to being an allergist, either a board-certified internist or a board-certified pediatrician. In consulting a board-certified allergist, you can be confident you are dealing with an individual who has proven qualifications.

QUESTIONS TO ASK YOUR NEW DOCTOR

In learning about the doctor you are planning to consult, you shouldn't be bashful about asking the following questions:

- Where did you go to medical school?
- Where did you do your internship and fellowship?
- Are you board certified?

If you cannot get independent assurances of the quality of the medical training (such as board certifications), we recommend that you seek another doctor.

SEEKING THE ADVICE OF A SECOND DOCTOR: Perhaps the most likely situation in which you will need to seek the advice of another doctor is when your own doctor recommends it. Special problems often require special treatments; in such cases, your doctor will formally refer you to a specialist and his or her staff will probably arrange for an appointment.

There are other instances when you may feel the need for a second opinion from another doctor. There are a few simple guidelines to help you determine when you should change doctors (see below), but the most fundamental one is a matter of basic psychology: if you feel uncomfortable with the care you or your child is getting, for whatever reason, and you have been unable to receive satisfactory answers or advice from the doctor when you have expressed your concerns, then it may be prudent to seek another opinion or another doctor.

WHEN TO SEEK THE ADVICE OF A SECOND DOCTOR

- If there has been no improvement in the first three to six months of treatment.
- If you or your child has had to go to a hospital emergency room more than once in any one year for an asthmatic episode, or if you or your child has had to be hospitalized more than once in the past two years.
- If your doctor is unable to give you the detailed explanations you need about the course of treatment.
- If oral steroids are used on a daily basis.

OTHER ISSUES: In order for you, your child, and your doctor to establish the best possible relationship, there are several issues on which you should reach an understanding.

Cost: There is much to learn about the disease from the doctor; the cost of the treatment is one of them. Treatment is often costly, yet many people find it difficult to discuss money with their doctor. Although costs will vary depending on the type of treatment, it's important that you come to some understanding of what the cost will be beginning on day one. Any disagreement over money later can lead to distrust and a possible break in the relationship—which can mean increased stress for the patient as well as a loss of time and money.

Referrals: It is a common practice for one doctor to refer a patient to another. There are several reasons why a referral is made. For example, your doctor may want a second opinion, or he or she may suspect a problem another doctor may be better qualified to treat.

In such cases, your concern must be to learn who will be in charge. Which doctor is making the decisions about treatment, and who will continue to maintain control of the day-to-day management of the disease? It's conceivable that the doctor you are referred to may want to assume complete responsibility for management of the asthma; alternatively, he or she may act only as a one-time consultant.

Emergencies: Emergencies are not uncommon, particularly for children with long-term asthma. If a visit to the emergency room or hospitalization is necessary, you'll need to know who to call at one o'clock in the morning—find out if your doctor or another doctor is available day and night. If your doctor is in a group practice, will the other doctor(s) be familiar with your situation? With what hospital is your doctor affiliated? What hospital does he or she recommend if your child has an emergency? Is it a teaching hospital—one connected to a medical school—so there will be several interns and residents on call?

Treatment Approach: It is not important that you decide initially what is the best approach for your care or the care of your child, but it is important that you know what your doctor has in mind.

There are various ways of treating a patient with asthma, and each involves different goals. One doctor may choose lots of medication to get you or your child free of any abnormal lung function; another may choose less medication even if some mild symptoms remain. What is important, again, is that you have reached an understanding with the doctor about what can be accomplished and how.

In summary, be sure to ask all the questions you need to; otherwise your doctor may assume that you already know the answers. Don't be afraid to ask a question more than once and write the answer down if it's important. If you keep a diary, write down all the things you want to discuss with your doctor before your visit (see page 119). That shows respect for his or her time and yours.

Progress in the treatment of asthma can be uneven, but in most cases you should expect to see steady improvement. You may never be totally free of symptoms, but the attacks should grow less frequent and less severe. If you go through a period when the asthma seems to get worse despite treatment, ask your doctor about it. If you feel comfortable with him or her, you should be able to tell him or her that you are concerned and would like to seek another opinion; in that situation, you should ask for a referral. That's all part of the communication you wanted when you selected the doctor.

Talking to the Doctor by Telephone in an Emergency

Whether you are calling a doctor for yourself or your child, the rules are the same if the problem is urgent. Keep calm and patiently explain the situation. You may find it easier to talk with your own doctor, but if you can't reach him or her and you call the hospital, the doctor there requires the same information.

The fact is, the medical guidance you get will be based largely on the information you provide over the telephone. The following guidelines will be helpful to you and the doctor during an emergency.

Give your name and age (or your child's name and age). Explain why you are calling and what you think the problem is.

Be prepared to describe clearly what symptoms you (or your child) has. An unfamiliar doctor will want to know when you (or the child) was last seen by a doctor for treatment of asthma.

Be prepared to give the doctor the name of any medications prescribed for treating the asthma, and how much and how recently a dose was taken.

ESSENTIAL FACTS FOR THE DOCTOR

Review the following checklist to identify what symptoms you (or your child) may be experiencing:

Fast, irregular, or noisy and difficult breathing
Wheezing, coughing, or tightness in the chest
Flared nostrils when breathing in
Pursed lips when breathing out
Blueness of the lips, nail beds, or skin
No breathing sounds at all (fixed chest)
Restlessness at night, inability to sleep
Concavity (inward curving) at the base of the throat or between the ribs
Inability to sit or stand up straight
Hunched posture
Unusual paleness
Tiny pupils of eyes
Rapid heartbeat
Vomiting
Fatigue
Fidgetiness
Anxiety or fear
Diarrhea
Excess mucus (cite the color and amount)
Headache
Postnasal drip
Heartburn

If you've already tried everything your doctor advises before you called, say so. If the doctor tells you not to go to the hospital but to stay home and follow certain instructions, do so. If there are no positive results within a reasonable length of time, call the doctor again. Preferably, arrange for a time to call back in the possibility that you (or your child) does not improve.

Insist on clear instructions. Your welfare (or that of your child) depends on it. If the doctor speaks too fast, ask him or her to speak more slowly. If the doctor uses language or words you don't understand, ask for an explanation. Everything depends on your understanding the instructions.

HELPING YOUR CHILD COPE

When your child is suffering an asthmatic episode, try to follow these guidelines:

- Speak quietly to your child; calm him or her down. Try not to reveal your own anxiety.
- Remind your child of breathing and relaxation exercises (see pages 135 and 136).
- Do any physical therapy techniques you've been trained to use to drain the lungs of mucus.

The Medical History

The most important part of the opening phase of the patient/doctor relationship is the medical history that the doctor obtains from the patient. That history should include a careful documentation of the onset of the disease, its pattern (with a particular emphasis on the time of day or night, the circumstances surrounding the onset, and the frequency of the symptoms), the effect the disease has had on the patient's life and lifestyle, the frequency of emergency room visits and hospitalizations, the medications taken, and the manner in which the patient tolerates his or her disease (that is, the emotional response to the asthma).

Many of these questions must be gone into in detail because they have implications as to the asthma's causes. For example, if you have any symptoms at night, your doctor will want to know precisely what time of night and how many hours after you have gone to bed they occur. Your doctor will ask if the symptoms include wheezing or coughing and whether the attacks are associated with postnasal drip, sneezing, nasal congestion, or heartburn. He or she may also ask whether attacks are relieved by standing, coughing, or medication.

Recording all the facets of the history will take between thirty minutes and an hour. In addition to the patient/doctor interview, which is the most important part of the history taking, you may be given a standardized questionnaire to help your doctor fill in some of the gaps that the interview might have missed.

The importance of a comprehensive and detailed history cannot be exaggerated, as the entire asthma treatment is based on it. Since the data provides the doctor with most of the information he or she needs to arrive at a proper diagnosis or to decide upon further diagnostic tests, you may need to expand on many points of your history. The doctor needs to be satisfied that he or she has the best possible understanding of what needs to be treated.

SYMPTOMS: Many questions will focus on the pattern of the symptoms. Are they sudden or gradual? Do they disappear quickly after using an inhaler? Do the symptoms involve mucus and, if so, how much and what is the stickiness or thickness of it? Are the symptoms associated with infections and, if so, what sort of infections, bacterial or viral? Do you have any warning before the symptoms develop? Do you have time to treat your asthma before it gets worse? If you have an asthma attack, how long does it last? How long before you come back to normal?

TALKING TO YOUR DOCTOR: THE QUESTIONS

The following are some of the questions the doctor may ask that would more clearly indicate asthma.

Do you experience . . .
- Wheezing in the chest upon breathing in or out?
- Shortness of breath?
- Coughing?
- Coughing and wheezing together?
- Coughing that produces mucus? If so, how much mucus and how thick is it? Is the mucus clear, yellow, or greenish?
- Tightness in the chest?
- A tickle in the throat that leads to coughing?
- Postnasal drip?

DRUGS: Your doctor will want to know what drugs you have been taking and how well they have worked. What sort of side effects have you had with the drugs? What other drugs have you tried, and were they useful treatments? What other drugs are you taking now that are unrelated to your asthma?

ALLERGIES: If you have allergies, are they seasonal? What allergens are you exposed to? Is there a family history of allergies? Have you tried allergy shots and, if so, were they successful?

EMOTIONS: As we have discussed, factors that affect asthma are not restricted to what is inhaled or swallowed. Far more subtle issues that deal with the emotional state of the patient at the time of the attack and aspects of the family history may be decisive in the choice of treatment. If the patient is a child, is he or she doing well at school? Does he or she get along with his peers? Do symptoms occur mostly at school or at home? If the patient is an adult, do symptoms follow shortly after episodes of emotional stress?

TALKING TO YOUR DOCTOR: THE ANSWERS

The following are activities, conditions, and substances that are known to cause asthma symptoms. Your doctor needs to learn whether you associate any of your symptoms with any of the items on this list.

- Animals
- Change of residence
- Cold weather
- Damp weather
- Dust exposure
- Excitement
- Fatigue
- Foods
- Medications
- Aspirin
- Laughter
- Heartburn
- Exercise
- Frustration
- Hot weather
- Insect bites
- Plants or grass
- Rainy weather
- Tension
- Travel
- Windy weather
- Birth control pills
- Tranquilizers
- Sinusitis
- Work or occupational exposure
- Specific times of the day or night
- Upper respiratory tract infections or colds
- Tobacco smoke or other irritant exposure

ENVIRONMENT: Your doctor will ask you about your house and your workplace to determine sources of allergens or irritants which you may be inhaling on a regular basis. Many things can trigger asthma or make it worse, particularly dust, animal hair, and molds.

TALKING TO YOUR DOCTOR: THE SENSITIVITIES

Your doctor will want to know where you live and work, and if you are aware of any sensitivity to certain allergens. To that end, he or she may ask you some of the following questions:

- How long have you lived at the present location?
- What type of heat does your house have (gas, oil, or electric)?
- What type of air conditioning (central or room units)?
- Are there cigarette, cigar, or pipe smokers?
- Do you use a humidifier?
- Are there any animals in the house? Where do they sleep?
- Are there any plants? Where are they located?
- Are there cockroaches?
- What type of floor coverings do you have in the bedroom?
- What type of padding is there under the rug or carpet (natural or synthetic fiber)?
- What materials are bedroom drapes, curtains, shades, or shutters made of?
- What kind of mattress, box spring, and dust-proof cover do you use?
- What kinds of blankets, quilts, or bedspreads do you use?
- What type of pillows do you use (feather or synthetic foam)?
- Do you have books on open bookshelves?
- Is there stuffed furniture or toys around the room?
- Are there any wall hangings?

(A detailed explanation of the significance of these items in your home can be found on page 82.)

FAMILY HISTORY: Since it is believed that the tendency to develop asthma runs in families, the doctor will want to know whether there is any family history of asthma or allergies. He or she will also want to know if anyone has skin disorders, hay fever, persistent sinus infections, nasal polyps, or any respiratory diseases such as chronic colds, pneumonia, or tuberculosis. When speaking of your "family," keep in mind that your doctor is concerned with any member of your immediate family, as well as maternal and paternal grandparents, cousins, aunts, and uncles.

The doctor will want to know much about your personal health as part of this medical history. In addition to any history of heart, liver, or blood pressure problems, he or she will be especially concerned with childhood diseases. It is also important for the doctor to know if you think you might be pregnant.

For children, the doctor should know facts about early growth and development, such as feeding problems, episodes of bronchitis or pneumonia, and immunization records.

The Physical Examination

Next comes a careful and thorough physical examination. Special attention will be paid to those signs associated with allergies.

THE NOSE: In addition to examining the eyes and ears, your doctor will carefully look for signs of allergies in the nose. He or she will be concerned with any evidence of sinusitis, nasal polyps, or structural abnormalities in the nose that could cause sinusitis. These abnormalities would include large spurs or growths on the bone that could interfere with draining from the sinuses, like the presence of enlarged turbinate bones obstructing the sinuses. The doctor will also look for any foreign objects in the nose which could be related to your symptoms.

THE CHEST: When examining the chest, the doctor will carefully monitor the pattern of breathing, especially if there is use of accessory muscles of respiration not ordinarily employed during quiet breathing. He or she will look to see if both sides of the chest move evenly during breathing; an imbalance suggests an obstruction. The doctor will also check the diaphragm muscle for any irregular movement.

When the doctor listens to the chest, it's to learn if there is any obstruction of airflow. Besides listening for wheezing, he or she is concerned about "rhonchi," rattling or gravellike sounds, which would indicate the presence of mucus along the airway. If wheezing is present, the doctor may perform a pulmonary function test, give the patient an inhaler bronchodilator, and repeat the test to determine whether the wheezing improves after use of the bronchodilator (page 42).

Beyond the examination of the thyroid gland to ascertain its size and assure there are no enlargements or associated tumors, the balance of the examination will resemble a general overall physical examination.

Into
the
Laboratory

Depending on the findings of the physical examination and the symptoms you have experienced, your doctor is likely to order a number of tests.

In Chapter 1 we saw that some diseases look like or mimic asthma. If your doctor has some reason to believe that your symptoms are not the result of asthma but of some other illness, he or she may order some appropriate laboratory tests to help make a diagnosis. However, even if your doctor is quite confident that asthma is your problem, tests may be needed to determine the severity of the disease, the damage it may have caused to lung function, the possible triggers or "causes" that are responsible for some of the symptoms, the possibility of other risk factors such as heart or blood vessel damage, or whether you might suffer any adverse effects from certain medications.

Pulmonary Function Tests

Asthma can affect the ability of the bronchial tubes or airways of the lungs to take in and expel air. Pulmonary function tests are used to determine whether asthma is the correct diagnosis and, if so, the extent of the disability caused by the asthma.

THE SPIROMETER: The simplest of these tests is called spirometry and, appropriately, it's performed on a device called a spirometer (from *spirare,* to breathe, and *metron,* to measure). There's nothing complicated about its use. Patients practice breathing through its mouthpiece until they feel comfortable. When they feel relaxed with the device, they are instructed to take the deepest possible breath and to exhale the air as quickly and completely as possible. The volume of air that is collected in the first second of exhalation in relation to the total lung volume is a measure of lung function.

The spirometer allows the doctor to determine whether there is blockage of airflow (obstruction) in the airways. If airflow obstruction is present, the doctor will often repeat the test after giving the patient a bronchodilator, a drug that opens (dilates) constricted airways. In many asthma patients, the airflow obstruction can be rapidly reversed with proper bronchodilators. If the drug works, it confirms that the airflow obstruction is not permanent and indicates that bronchodilators will likely be successful therapy for that patient.

However, if the obstruction of airflow does not respond to bronchodilators, the diagnosis of asthma may be questioned, and more consideration will have to be given to the possibility that bronchitis or some chronic obstructive airway disease is present. Emphysema, which is a chronic obstructive disease of the alveoli, might be suspected because it causes airflow obstruction but is not affected by bronchodilators.

Finally, many physicians find that pulmonary function testing provides a useful standard for indicating successful therapy in patients. Therefore, it's very common for patients with asthma to have spirometry with and without bronchodilators on every visit to their doctor's office.

Bronchial Provocation Tests

For people with asthmatic symptoms who have normal pulmonary function tests, a bronchial provocation test may be in order. It is also useful for people who have variations of asthma symptoms, like a chronic cough but no wheezing.

In a bronchial provocation test, the patient is asked to breathe in substances, such as methacholine or histamines, either of which will cause asthmatics to develop mild wheezing. Since these substances rarely affect nonasthmatics, the absence of a response is regarded as a clear indication that asthma is not the problem.

Blood Tests

A blood test, which involves taking a small sample of blood, usually two vials, for study, can yield some very important information.

An analysis of a small sample can disclose the number of red blood cells present and the amount of hemoglobin, the iron-containing pigment of the red blood cells, available to transport oxygen. An elevated red blood cell count reveals a condition in which the level of oxygen in the circulating blood has been reduced; that shortfall of oxygen stimulates the bone marrow to produce more red blood cells to carry the limited amount of available oxygen to the tissues. Improper ventilation will often be the cause of an elevated red blood cell count.

In some cases, especially in an acute episode of asthma, it is important to learn the amount of oxygen and carbon dioxide in the blood. Measuring the amount of this gas in the blood is useful in determining how well someone's been able to remove carbon dioxide from the lungs. This blood test, called arterial blood gases, is also important because if the carbon dioxide reaches a certain level, it can make the blood toxic and seriously threaten the life of the patient.

Arterial blood gases should be measured in people who have severe asthma and who have failed to respond to therapy within a thirty-minute time limit, in people in severe distress, or in those with a history of frequent hospitalizations for asthma or multiple emergency room visits in the preceding hours or days.

Chest X Ray

An X ray looks like the negative of a photograph, but the content of the photograph is the interior rather than the exterior appearance of the body part that is being x-rayed. X rays emitted by an X-ray tube pass unimpeded through air-filled structures and turn photographic film black when they strike it. In contrast, these X rays are absorbed when they strike solid structures; therefore, the object that absorbed the X ray appears white on the film.

X rays are of limited value in determining the diagnosis or severity of an acute attack of asthma. Unless there is some object blocking the lungs, they will usually appear normal. However, X rays are helpful in evaluating complications such as rib fractures and pneumonia, which can occur in patients with severe asthma. It is recommended that X rays of the sinuses be considered in patients with persistent runny and inflamed noses and sinuses, especially if they complain a great deal of nasal congestion, persistent sinus headaches, or frequent and recurring upper respiratory tract infections.

Skin Testing

Allergy skin tests are the most effective and rapid diagnostic tests to determine an individual's sensitivity to specific allergens. Allergy skin tests can be done in a few minutes in an allergist's office. They are safe, almost painless, and provide rapid confirmation of any suspected allergens.

Allergens that can be identified by skin testing include all airborne allergens, such as pollens, dust, and molds. In addition, skin testing can be used to determine allergies to stinging insect venoms, foods, and many other environmental substances, as well as to certain drugs, such as penicillin and penicillin derivatives. However, many drugs are not discernible by skin testing since allergies develop from the metabolites of the drug (substances created after the drug has undergone chemical changes in the body) and not the drug itself. Skin testing is also thought to be of little use for patients with hives alone because hives usually are not caused by allergies.

Skin tests can be useful in confirming as allergens those substances that have come under suspicion because of the history you gave your doctor. For example, a patient who has certain seasonal or perennial symptoms and has a skin test that confirms them is considered to be allergic to the substances for which he or she tested positive. On the other hand, if a patient has no history of allergies but a positive skin test, the significance of the skin test has to be doubted. The point is that skin testing is only a confirmatory and not a diagnostic tool. If you don't have symptoms, it's not significant that your skin test was positive—at least not now. (Studies indicate that only about one in three of all patients with no allergy history who test positive later develop the disease.) So you needn't begin eliminating foods to which you have a positive skin test unless those foods cause symptoms. The bottom line: no symptoms, no problem.

You should be aware that it is the practice of some physicians to use RAST (see page 46) to make an allergy diagnosis, even in the absence of an allergy history. If the test is positive, they treat the patient for allergies. Like the skin test, however, RAST is to be regarded as no more than a confirmatory tool, and you should not enter into a program of allergy therapy based solely on RAST or a skin test.

There are several types of skin test. All involve exposing your tissue—either skin or blood—to potential allergens, and then observing the reaction. In a skin test, for example, the skin either reacts with a reddened inflammation (a positive response indicating you are allergic to the substance being tested) or it doesn't.

SCRATCH TEST: The procedure for the scratch test is simple: the doctor places a diluted drop of the allergen or suspected substance on your skin then scratches the skin's surface.

This procedure is the safest of the three skin tests since the allergen can be wiped away quickly if a severe reaction sets in. It is also the least painful of the skin tests, making it more tolerable to children.

PUNCTURE TEST: This test calls for the skin to be "tented" with a needlelike probe and a diluted amount of the allergen to be pushed under the hillock of skin.

This test is more sensitive than the scratch test and is less risky and uncomfortable than the intradermal or intracutaneous test (see below). For these reasons, it is often the preferred choice among the skin tests.

INTRADERMAL OR INTRACUTANEOUS TEST: With this technique the diluted allergen is injected between the layers of the skin. This is the most sensitive of the three skin tests, but it's more uncomfortable and poses a greater risk because the doctor can't wipe the solution away if a severe allergic reaction develops.

RAST (Radioallergosorbent Test)

This test, usually part of the blood-testing procedure, measures the amount of chemicals in your body that set off allergic reactions. It is expensive, but it is the safest of the allergy tests. However, it is also the least sensitive.

RAST is controversial because some doctors rely on it too heavily for diagnosis. Once again, understanding your allergies requires a thorough medical history, careful observation on your part, and perhaps even an elimination diet (in which you eliminate those foods you suspect for a period and later reintroduce them into your diet, being watchful for allergic reactions). These other considerations are more important than any one test.

Medication

The key to any asthma treatment program is proper medication—medication taken faithfully and correctly.

It is very important that you precisely follow your doctor's instructions regarding the dosage and timing of your medication. Out of a mistaken belief that more is better, many patients increase the dosage of the drugs their doctor has prescribed. To either increase the dosage of your medication or take it more frequently may increase the side effects and cause dangerous medical problems.

The side effects from long-term or excessive use of some asthma medications range from risk of ulcers and cataracts to retarded growth in children. Therefore, stick to the medication program your doctor prescribed. By doing so, you may not only reduce the impact of asthma in your daily life, but you may reduce the need for more or stronger medications such as oral steroids, which have the potential for producing even more serious side effects if they must be relied on for any extended period.

KNOW YOUR DRUGS: The informed asthma patient knows how to deal with the sudden nature of his or her asthma episodes. Because asthma symptoms can occur without warning, it's important that you understand the medications, their proper use, their side effects, and the precautions you should take while using them.

In this section, we provide for each asthma drug a brief discussion of how it differs from the others; what its specific role in asthma care is; what you doctor must know from you before prescribing the specific medication; the most common side effects; the proper procedures for taking the drug; any dietary considerations related to taking the medication; and recommendations for proper storage.

The basic groups of drugs used for asthma are bronchodilators, theophylline, cromolyn, corticosteroids (steroids), antihistamines, and ipratropium. On occasion, patients may use expectorants, decongestants, and perhaps a variety of cold remedy preparations. With the exception of corticosteroids, any one of these drugs can be prescribed as the first choice for treating asthma. Corticosteroids are frequently not given initially for the treatment of asthma because they can produce significant and troubling side effects, but they may be added later. For example, oral corticosteroids are usually prescribed when maximum tolerated dosages of the other medications are found to be inadequate to control asthma symptoms.

In reading about and discussing drugs, it is important to know the difference between generic and brand names. The generic is the name a drug is given at its first discovery or concoction in a laboratory. It identifies the drug's unique chemistry and distinguishes it from all others. When that generic is marketed, however, it is given another name, a brand name.

When the Food and Drug Administration approves a drug for sale and use, generally one drug manufacturer has developed it and is licensed to sell it. The drug is then sold under a brand name, but with its generic name cited on the package as well. A number of years after its release, however, a drug becomes public property and other manufacturers can sell it also. At that point, there are likely to be a number of brand names under which the drug is sold. To make matters more complicated still, some manufacturers may sell the drug under its generic name and not adorn it with a brand name. At a minimum, you should know that the term ''generic'' describes drugs manufactured by more than one company, and as a result, these drugs generally are less expensive than brand names.

Not all drugs are administered the same way. Some are swallowed or inhaled; others can be administered by injection or, in some instances, rectally. In the following pages, we explain the advantages and disadvantages of the different forms of drugs.

INHALATION: Inhaling some medications can produce faster relief from asthma symptoms than taking them orally (by mouth) because the medication reaches the bronchial tubes directly and quickly. Consequently, inhalation is the most effective way to administer drugs in an emergency room, when relief is critical. In addition, inhalers or nebulizers are used in home inhalation programs for patients who have asthma that is unpredictable, severe, or generally difficult to manage.

The inhalation method is not difficult to learn, although procedures must be followed carefully. In brief, an inhalation treatment is prepared by placing a saline (salt) solution and the appropriate medication in the canister of a nebulizer. The patient then inhales the mist produced by the nebulizer, and an improvement in the patient's condition usually occurs within twenty minutes. The treatment can be repeated as often as every two hours, but treatment at intervals this frequent would call for the supervision of a doctor. At home, this inhalation treatment should not be repeated more than once every four to six hours without notifying your doctor. (See Chapter 4 for a detailed discussion of the proper use of a nebulizer and inhalation techniques in the home.)

Bronchodilators (Inhaled)

Bronchodilators are medicines that open up the bronchial tubes or air passages of the lungs. They can be inhaled, taken by mouth, or injected (see page 50). These drugs are sold under many generic names and even more brand names. For ease of discussion, we give the various forms of these drugs in general terms, since the action of the inhaled bronchodilators are much the same and their side effects are similar. Any significant differences are noted.

Generic Names: Albuterol, bitolterol, epinephrine, isoetharine, isoproterenol, metaproterenol, racepinephrine, and terbutaline.

Brand Names: Adrenalin, Aerolone, Alupent, Arm-a-Med Isoetharine, Arm-a-Med Isoproterenol, AsthmaHaler, AsthmaNefrin, Berotec, Beta-2, Brethaire, Bronitin Mist, Bronkaid Mist, Bronkaid Mistometer, Bronkaid Mist Suspension, Bronkometer, Bronkosol, Dey-Dose Isoetharine, Dey-Dose Isoproterenol, Dey-Dose Racepinephrine, Dey-Lute Isoetharine, Disorine, Dispos-a-Med Isoetharine, Dispos-a-Med Isoproterenol, Dysne-Inhal, Isuprel,

Isuprel Mistometer, Medihaler-Epi, Medihaler-Iso, Metaprel, microNefrin, Norisodrine Aerotrol, Primatene Mist Solution, Primatene Mist Suspension, Proventil, Salbutamol, S-2 Inhalant, Tornalate, Vapo-Iso, Vaponefrin, and Ventolin.

Effects: Acts on the nervous system to activate the muscles in the walls of bronchial tubes to expand them.

Prescribed For: Relief of difficult breathing associated with acute attacks of asthma.

What Your Doctor Must Know:

- If you believe you are allergic to albuterol, bitolterol, epinephrine, isoetharine, isoproterenol, metaproterenol, racepinephrine, terbutaline, any other inhalation medicines, or to sulfites or other preservatives.
- If you are pregnant, planning to become pregnant, or are breast-feeding.
- If you have a history of heart or blood vessel disease, high blood pressure, an overactive thyroid, or diabetes mellitus.
- (To take epinephrine) If you have a history of brain damage, mental disease, or Parkinson's disease.
- (To take bitolterol or terbutaline) If you have a seizure disorder (or history of).
- If you are using any of the other bronchodilators (listed above), or any other medication, whether prescribed or over-the-counter, such as amphetamines, high blood pressure medications, appetite supressants, beta-blockers, caffeine, chlophedianol, heart medicine, diuretics, levodopa, methylphenidate, nitrates, pemoline, thyroid hormones; anything for the eye such as betaxolol, levobunolol, or timolol; and any medicine for colds, sinus problems, or hay fever.

Side Effects: Inhaled bronchodilators can cause nervousness, restlessness, and trembling. Some of these medications will temporarily cause a bad taste in the mouth, and isoproterenol may cause the saliva to turn pinkish to red. Less frequent side effects are coughing, dizziness or light-headedness, drowsiness, dryness of the mouth or throat (rinsing with water after each dose may help), flushing or redness of the face or skin, headaches, a mild increase in blood pressure, muscle cramp or twitching, nausea or vomiting, troubled sleep, sweating, accelerated heartbeat, unusual paleness, and weakness. These side effects usually do not require medical attention unless they persist.

Overdose: Symptoms are discomfort or pain in the chest, chills or fever, headaches, dizziness or light-headedness, sharp increase or decrease in blood pressure, muscle cramps, nausea or vomiting, seizures, shortness of breath, trembling, unusual anxiety, nervousness or restlessness, unusually fast or slow heartbeat, unusually large pupils or blurred vision, unusual paleness or coldness of the skin, and chronic weakness. These side effects require a doctor's attention as soon as possible.

Proper Use: Keep the spray away from the eyes because it may cause irritation. Don't use epinephrine, isoetharine, or isoproterenol if the solution turns pinkish to brownish in color or if it becomes cloudy.

Dosage: Do not take more than two inhalations at any one time unless otherwise directed by your doctor. If you are also using the inhalation aerosol form of an adrenocorticoid (cortisonelike medicine, such as beclomethasone, dexamethasone, flunisolide, or triamcinolone), allow five minutes between applications of the bronchodilator and the adrenocorticoid, unless otherwise directed by your doctor. If you are using an inhaled bronchodilator in an aerosol form and you use all of the medicine in one canister in less than two weeks, check with your doctor. You may be using too much medicine.

How To Store: Store away from heat. Store the aerosol form away from direct sunlight. Do not puncture, break, or burn the aerosol container, even if it is empty.

Bronchodilators (Taken by Mouth or Injected)

Bronchodilators are medicines that open up the bronchial tubes or air passages of the lungs. They may be taken by mouth or given by injection to treat the symptoms of bronchial asthma. Some forms of these medicines can be inhaled (see page 48.)

These drugs come under several generic names and many brand names. As with the inhaled bronchodilators, we discuss all the generic brands of this drug together, since the action and side effects of the bronchodilators that are taken by mouth or injected are much the same. Any significant differences are noted.

Generic Names: Albuterol, ephedrine, epinephrine, ethylnorepinephrine, fenoterol, isoproterenol, metaproterenol, and terbutaline.

Brand Names: Adrenal, Alupent, Berotec, Brethine, Bricanyl, Bronkephrine, EpiPen, EpiPen Jr., Isuprel, Metaprel, Proventil, Salbutamool, Sus-Phrine, and Ventolin.

Effects: Acts on the nervous system to relax the muscles in the walls of bronchial tubes to open them up and reduce swelling.

Prescribed For: Relief of difficult breathing associated with acute attacks of asthma.

What Your Doctor Must Know:

- If you believe you are allergic to albuterol, ephedrine, epinephrine, ethylnorepinephrine, fenoterol, isoproterenol, metaproterenol, terbutaline, any foods, or to sulfites or other preservatives.
- If you are pregnant, planning to become pregnant, or are breast-feeding.
- If you are on a low-salt, low-sugar, or any other special diet.
- If you have a history of heart or blood vessel disease, high blood pressure, an overactive thyroid, or diabetes mellitus.
- (To take epinephrine) If you have a history of brain damage, mental disease, Parkinson's disease, or an enlarged prostate.
- (To take terbutaline) If you have a seizure disorder (or history of).
- If you are using any of the other bronchodilators (listed above), or any other medication, whether prescribed or over-the-counter, such as amantadine, amphetamines, high blood pressure medicine, appetite suppressants, beta-blockers, caffeine, chlophedianol, heart medicine, diuretics, levodopa, methylphenidate, nitrates, pemoline, thyroid hormones; anything for the eye such as betaxolol, levobunolol, or timolol; or any medicine for colds, sinus problems, or hay fever.

Side Effects: Bronchodilators that are taken by mouth or injected can cause nervousness, restlessness, and trembling. While using albuterol, fenoterol, metaproterenol, or terbutaline, you may experience temporarily a bad taste in the mouth, and isoproterenol may cause the saliva to turn pinkish to red. Less frequent side effects are difficult or painful urination, dizziness or light-headedness, drowsiness, dryness of the mouth or throat (rinsing with water after each dose may help), flushing or redness of the face or skin, headaches, heartburn, a mild increase in blood pressure, muscle cramp or twitching, nausea or vomiting, troubled sleep, sweating, accelerated heartbeat, unusual paleness, and weakness. These side effects usually do not require medical attention unless they persist.

Overdose: Symptoms are bluish coloration of the skin, discomfort or pain in the chest, chills or fever, headaches, dizziness or light-headedness, sharp increase or decrease in blood pressure, muscle cramps, nausea or vomiting, seizures, shortness of breath, trembling, unusual anxiety, nervousness or restlessness, unusually fast or slow heartbeat, unusually large pupils or blurred vision, unusual paleness or coldness of the skin, and chronic weakness. These side effects require a doctor's attention as soon as possible.

Proper Use: If you are using the epinephrine autoinjector (automatic injection device), it is important that you not remove the safety cap on the autoinjector until you are ready to use it. This prevents accidental activation of the device during storage and handling. To use the epinephrine autoinjector:

- Remove the safety cap.
- Place the tip on the thigh, at a right angle to the leg.
- Press hard into the thigh until the autoinjector functions. Hold in place for several seconds. Then remove the autoinjector and discard.
- Massage the injection area for ten seconds.

If you have any questions about how to give yourself injections, check with your doctor before proceeding.

Do not chew or swallow isoproterenol sublingual tablets. This medicine is meant to be absorbed through the lining of the mouth. Place a tablet under your tongue (sublingual) and let it slowly dissolve there. Do not swallow until the tablet has dissolved completely.

Dosage: Use the medicine as directed. Do not take larger doses or use more often than recommended on the label unless otherwise directed by your doctor. If you are using this medicine regularly and you miss a dose, use it as soon as possible. Then use any remaining doses for that day at regularly spaced intervals. Do not double dose.

How To Store: Store away from heat. Store the capsule or table form of this medicine away from direct light. Do not store the capsule in the bathroom medicine cabinet because heat and moisture may cause the medicine to break down. Store the suspension form of epinephrine injection in the refrigerator, but keep it from freezing. Do not keep outdated medicine. Flush expired capsules, syrup, or tablet forms of this medicine down the toilet unless otherwise directed.

Bronchodilators (Xanthine Derivatives)

Bronchodilators derived from a chemical known as xanthine are medicines that open up the bronchial tubes or air passages of the lungs to relieve coughing, wheezing, shortness of breath, and troubled breathing. They are taken by mouth, given by injection, or used rectally. The liquid, uncoated (chewable) tablet, capsule, and rectal enema dosage forms may be used for the treatment of acute asthma attacks or for long-term treatment of asthma. Rectal enemas should not be used for longer than forty-eight hours because they may irritate the rectum. The coated tablet and extended-release dosage forms are usually used only for long-term treatment. Generally, aminophylline rectal suppositories are not recommended because they are poorly absorbed.

Of these drugs, the most commonly used in the treatment of asthma is theophylline. Theophylline, as well as the other medicines, is available in long-acting and short-acting forms, and your doctor will prescribe one or the other depending on whether you need medication on a daily basis or only occasionally.

Your doctor will tell you whether your medication is long-acting or short-acting. However, many of the long-acting products can be recognized by designations such as "CRT" (controlled-release), "LA" (long-acting), "SA" (sustained-action), or "SR" (slow release). The advantage of a long-acting medication is that you don't have to take the drug as often.

Generic Names: Aminophylline, dyphylline, oxtriphylline, theophylline, and theophylline sodium glycinate.

Brand Names: There are more than seventy brand names. A complete list of these can be found in the book *Drug Information for the Consumer* (see Chapter 5). Brand names include Accurbron, Bronkodyl, Constant-T, Droxine, Droxine L.A., Duraphyl, Dyflex, Elixicon, Liquophylline, Neothylline, Somophyllin, Theo-24, Theobid Duracaps, Theolair, Theon, Theo-Time, Truphylline, and Uniphyl.

Effects: Relaxes the muscles of the bronchial tubes.

Prescribed For: Relief of difficult breathing associated with acute and chronic attacks of asthma.

What Your Doctor Must Know:

- If you believe you are allergic to aminophylline, caffeine, dyphylline, ethylenediamine (contained in animophylline), oxtriphylline, theobromine, or theophylline.
- If you are pregnant, planning to become pregnant, or are breast-feeding.
- If you have diarrhea, an enlarged prostate, fibrocystic breast disease, heart disease, or stomach ulcer (or a history of) or other stomach problems.

- If you are taking cortisonelike medicines, amantadine, amphetamines, diet pills, beta-blockers, caffeine, chlophedianol, diarrhea medicine, lithium, methylphenidate, oral contraceptives containing estrogen, pemoline, levobunolol, or timolol; any other medicines for asthma or breathing problems; or any other prescription or nonprescription medicines, especially medicines for colds or allergies.
- (To take aminophylline, oxtriphylline, or theophylline) If you have a fever, liver disease, overactive thyroid, or a respiratory infection such as a flu; or if you are also taking allopurinol, barbiturates, carbamazepine, cimetidine, erythromycin, nicotine chewing gum or other medicine to help you stop smoking, phenytoin, primidone, rifampin, or troleandomycin; or if you are going to receive a vaccine, smoke or have smoked regularly within the last two years (this affects the amount of medicine you may need), or are on a low-protein, high-carbohydrate diet or a high-protein, low-carbohydrate diet.

Side Effects: These drugs can cause nausea, nervousness, and restlessness, particularly among the elderly, infants, and those who are more sensitive to these medicines. The rectal medication infrequently may cause a burning or irritation of the rectum. These effects usually do not require medical attention and may go away during treatment as your body adjusts to the medicine. If they persist, check with your doctor.

Overdose: Symptoms are bloody or black tarry stools, confusion or change in behavior, diarrhea, dizziness or light-headedness, flushing or redness of the face, headache, increased urination, irritability, loss of appetite, muscle twitching, nausea or vomiting, seizures, stomach cramps or pain, trembling, troubled sleep, unusually fast breathing, pounding or irregular heartbeat, unusual tiredness or weakness, and vomiting blood or material that looks like coffee grounds. These side effects require a doctor's attention as soon as possible.

Proper Use: Do not change brands, forms, or dosage of this medicine without first checking with you doctor. If you refill your medicine and it looks different, check with your pharmacist. Different products may not work the same way.

If you are taking the once-a-day capsule or tablet form of this medicine, take one dose each morning after fasting overnight and at least one hour before eating. If you are taking chewable tablets, chew the tablets before swallowing. If you are taking coated tablets, swallow the tablets whole. Do not crush, break, or chew before swallowing. If you are taking extended-release capsules, swallow the capsule whole. Do not break (unless tablet is scored or marked for breaking), crush, or chew before swallowing. If you are taking aminophylline enema and you see that crystals have formed in the solution, dissolve them by placing the closed container of solution in warm water. Do not use the medicine if the crystals do not dissolve. All of these medicines should be taken in regularly spaced doses as directed by your doctor for maximum effect.

Dosage: If you miss a dose of this medicine, take it as soon as possible. However, if it is almost time for your next dose, skip the missed dose and go back to your regular schedule. Do not double dose.

Dietary Recommendations: Avoid eating or drinking large amounts of caffeine-containing foods or beverages such as chocolate, cocoa, tea, coffee, and cola drinks because they may add to an excessive stimulation of the central nervous system.

How To Store: Store away from heat and direct light. Do not store the capsule or tablet form in the bathroom medicine cabinet because heat and moisture may cause the medicine to break down. If you store it in the refrigerator, keep from freezing. If the medicine is outdated, flush the capsule, tablet, or liquid form down the toilet.

Theophylline, Ephedrine, and Barbiturates

Theophylline, ephedrine, and barbiturates can be combined in a liquid, tablet, or capsule form and taken orally to treat the symptoms of asthma or asthmatic bronchitis. Even though some of these medications are available without a prescription, it is advised that you follow your doctor's instruction as to their use in the treatment of asthma.

Brand Names: Azma Aid, Ephenyllin, Lardet, Phedral, Primatene "P" Formula, Tedral, Tedral SA, Tedrigen, T.E.P., Theocord, Theodrine, Theofed, Theofedral, Theophenyllin, and Theoral.

Effects: Acts on the nervous system to affect the muscles of the bronchial tubes and the small blood vessels (arterioles) in the tissues lining the respiratory passages.

Prescribed For: Relief of wheezing, coughing, shortness of breath, and troubled breathing associated with asthma.

What Your Doctor Must Know:

- If you believe you are allergic to aminophylline, caffeine, dyphylline, oxtriphylline, theobromine, theophylline, ephedrine, or medicines like ephedrine such as albuterol, amphetamines, epinephrine, isoproterenol, metaproterenol, norepinephrine, phenylephrine, phenylpropanoline, pseudoephedrine, or terbutaline; barbiturates; any foods; sulfites or other preservatives; or dyes.

- If you are pregnant, planning to become pregnant, or are breast-feeding.
- If you are on a low-salt, low-sugar diet; a low-protein, high-carbohydrate diet, a high-protein, low-carbohydrate diet, or any other special diet.
- If you have diabetes mellitus, diarrhea, an enlarged prostate, fever, fibrocystic breast disease, heart or blood vessel disease, high blood pressure, hyperactivity (in children), kidney or liver disease, overactive thyroid, pain, porphyria (or a history of), respiratory infections, stomach ulcer (or history of) or other stomach problems, or an underactive adrenal gland.
- If you are taking any other prescription or nonprescription medicines, especially anticonvulsants (seizure medicine), antihistamines or medicine for hay fever or other allergies, barbiturates, cortisonelike medicines, medicine to thin the blood, beta-blockers, cimetidine, corticotropin, heart medicine, ergoloid mesylates, ergotamine, maprotiline, any medicine for asthma or breathing problems, muscle relaxants, narcotics, prescription pain medicine, sedatives, tranquilizers or sleeping medicine, tricyclic antidepressants, troleanodomycin.
- If you are now taking or have taken within the past two weeks monoamine oxidase (MAO) inhibitors, such as furazolidone, isocarboxazid, pargyline, phenelzine, procarbazine, tranylcypromine, or if you are going to receive a flu vaccine, smoke, or have smoked regularly within the last two years (this affects the amount of medicine you may need).

Side Effects: These drugs can cause drowsiness, headaches, nausea, nervousness, and restlessness and, less often, difficult or painful urination and a feeling of warmth, flushing, or redness of the face. These side effects are more likely to occur among elderly patients, who are more sensitive to these medicines. These effects usually do not require medical attention and may go away during treatment as your body adjusts to the medicine. If they persist, check with your doctor.

Overdose: Symptoms are bloody or black tarry stools, chest pain, diarrhea, dizziness or light-headedness, hallucinations (seeing, hearing, or feeling things that are not there), irritability, loss of appetite, mood or mental changes, muscle twitching, nausea or vomiting, seizures, stomach cramps or pain, trembling, troubled sleep, unusual increase or decrease in blood pressure, unusually fast or irregular heartbeat, unusual tiredness or weakness, or vomiting blood or material that looks like coffee grounds. These side effects require a doctor's attention as soon as possible.

Proper Use: For this medicine to be quick acting, it is best that you take it with a glass of water on an empty stomach either one hour before meals or two hours after meals. If the medicine upsets your stomach, your doctor may suggest taking it with meals to reduce irritation. Because drowsiness may occur, make sure you know how you will react to this medicine before you drive, use machines, or do other jobs that require you to be alert.

Dosage: This medicine must be taken every day in regularly spaced doses. If you miss a dose, take it as soon as possible. However, if it is almost time for your next dose, skip the missed dose and go back to your regular schedule. Do not double dose.

Dietary Recommendations: Avoid eating or drinking large amounts of caffeine-containing foods or beverages such as chocolate, cocoa, tea, coffee, and cola drinks because they may add to an excessive stimulation of the central nervous system. Do not eat carbohydrate-rich foods and charcoal-broiled foods regularly because these may make the medicine less effective.

How To Store: Store away from heat and direct light. Do not store the capsule or tablet form in the bathroom medicine cabinet because the heat and moisture may cause the medicine to break down. If you store it in the refrigerator, keep from freezing. If the medicine is outdated, flush the capsule, tablet, or liquid form down the toilet.

Theophylline, Ephedrine, and Hydroxyzine

Theophylline, ephedrine, and hydroxyzine can be combined in a liquid, tablet, or capsule form and taken orally to treat the symptoms of asthma or asthmatic bronchitis. Unlike the combination drugs containing theophylline, ephedrine, and barbiturates (page 55), some of which are available without a prescription, these drugs cannot be purchased without a doctor's prescription.

Brand Names: Brophed, Hydrophed, Hydrophed D.F., Marax, Marax D.F., Moxy Compound, T.E.H. Compound, and Theozine.

Effects: Acts on the nervous system to affect the muscles of the bronchial tubes and the small blood vessels (arterioles) in the tissues lining the respiratory passages.

Prescribed For: Relief of wheezing, coughing, shortness of breath, and troubled breathing associated with asthma.

What Your Doctor Must Know:

- If you believe you are allergic to aminophylline, caffeine, dyphylline, hydroxyzine, oxtriphylline, theobromine, theophylline, ephedrine, or medicines like ephedrine such as albuterol, amphetamines, epinephrine, isoproterenol, metaproterenol, norepinephrine, phenylephrine, phenylpropanolamine, pseudoephedrine, or terbutaline; any foods; sulfites or other preservatives; or dyes.
- If you are pregnant, planning to become pregnant, or are breast-feeding.
- If you are on low-salt, low-sugar diet; a low-protein, high-carbohydrate diet; a high-protein, low-carbohydrate diet, or any other special diet.
- If you have diabetes mellitus, diarrhea, an enlarged prostate, fever, fibrocystic breast disease, heart or blood vessel disease, high blood pressure, hyperactivity (in children), liver disease, overactive thyroid, respiratory infections, or stomach ulcer (or history of) or other stomach problems.
- If you are taking any other prescription or nonprescription medicines, especially anticonvulsants (seizure medicine), antihistamines or medicine for hay fever or other allergies, barbiturates, beta-blockers, cimetidine, heart medicine, ergoloid mesylates, ergotamine, erythromycin, maprotiline, any medicine for asthma or breathing problems, muscle relaxants, narcotics, prescription pain medicine, sedatives, tranquilizers or sleeping medicine, tricyclic antidepressants, or troleandomycin.
- If you are now taking or have taken within the past two weeks monoamine oxidase (MAO) inhibitors, such as furazolidone, isocarboxazid, pargyline, phenelzine, procarbazine, tranylcypromine, or if you are going to receive a flu vaccine, smoke, or have smoked regularly within the last two years (this affects the amount of medicine you may need).

Side Effects: These drugs can cause drowsiness, headaches, nausea, nervousness, and restlessness and, less often, difficult or painful urination or a feeling of warmth or redness of the face. These side effects are more likely to occur among the elderly patients, who are more sensitive to these medicines. These effects usually do not require medical attention and may go away during treatment as your body adjusts to the medicine. If they persist, check with your doctor. If you develop symptoms of a flu or a fever, check with your doctor. These conditions may increase the risk of side effects.

Overdose: Symptoms are bloody or black tarry stools, chest pain, diarrhea, dizziness or light-headedness, hallucinations (seeing, hearing, or feeling things that are not there), irritability, loss of appetite, mood or mental changes, muscle twitching, nausea or vomiting, seizures, stomach cramps or pain, trembling, and troubled sleep. These side effects require a doctor's attention as soon as possbile.

Proper Use: For this medicine to be quick acting, it is best that you take it with a glass of water on an empty stomach either one hour before meals or two hours after meals. If the medicine upsets your stomach, your doctor may suggest taking it with meals to reduce irritation. For patients taking the extended-release tablet form of this medicine, swallow the tablet whole. Do not crush, break, or chew before swallowing. Because drowsiness may occur, make sure you know how you will react to this medicine before you drive, use machines, or do other jobs that require you to be alert.

Dosage: This medicine must be taken every day in regularly spaced doses. If you miss a dose, take it as soon as possible. However, if it is almost time for your next dose, skip the missed dose and go back to your regular schedule. Do not double dose.

Dietary Recommendations: Avoid eating or drinking large amounts of caffeine-containing foods or beverages such as chocolate, cocoa, tea, coffee, and cola drinks because they may add to an excessive stimulation of the central nervous system. Do not eat carbohydrate-rich foods and charcoal-broiled foods regularly because they may make the medicine less effective.

How To Store: Store away from heat and direct light. Do not store the capsule or tablet form in the bathroom medicine cabinet because heat and moisture may cause the medicine to break down. If you store it in the refrigerator, keep from freezing. If the medicine is outdated, flush the capsule, tablet, or liquid form down the toilet.

Theophylline and Guaifenesin

Theophylline and guaifenesin can be combined in a liquid, tablet, or capsule form and taken orally to treat the symptoms of asthma, chronic bronchitis, emphysema, and other lung diseases.

Brand Names: Asbron G, Asbron G (Inlay-Tabs), Bronchial, Elixophyllin-GG, Glyceryl T, Lanophyllin-GG, Quibron, Quiagen, Slo-Phyllin GG, Synophylate-GG, Theocolate, Theolair-Plus, and Theolate.

Effects: Acts on the muscles of the bronchial tubes to increase the flow of air.

Prescribed For: Relief of wheezing, coughing, shortness of breath, and troubled breathing associated with asthma.

What Your Doctor Must Know:

- If you believe you are allergic to aminophylline, caffeine, dyphylline, oxtriphylline, theobromine, theophylline, any foods, sulfites or other preservatives, or dyes.
- If you are pregnant, planning to become pregnant, or are breast-feeding.
- If you are on low-salt, low-sugar diet; a low-protein, high-carbohydrate diet; a high-protein, low-carbohydrate diet; or any other special diet.
- If you have diarrhea, an enlarged prostate, fever, fibrocystic breast disease, heart disease, liver disease, overactive thyroid, respiratory infections, or stomach ulcer (or history of) or other stomach problems.
- If you are taking any other prescription or nonprescription medicines, especially allopurinol, amantadine, amphetamines, appetite suppressants, barbiturates, beta-blockers, caffeine, carbamazepine, chlophedianol, cimetidine, diarrhea medicine containing kaolin or attapulgite, erythromycin, lithium, methylphenidate, nicotine chewing gum or other medicine to help you stop smoking, oral contraceptives containing estrogen, other medicine for asthma or breathing problems, pemoline, phenytoin, primidone, rifampin, troleandomycin, or any medicine for colds or allergies.
- If you are going to receive a flu vaccine, smoke, or have smoked regularly within the last two years (this affects the amount of medicine you may need.)

Side Effects: These drugs can cause nausea, nervousness, and restlessness. These side effects are more likely to occur among elderly patients, who are more sensitive to these medicines. These effects usually do not require medical attention and may go away during treatment as your body adjusts to the medicine. If they persist, check with your doctor. Less common are symptoms such as heartburn and vomiting. Check with your doctor when these side effects occur. If you develop symptoms of a flu or fever, see your doctor, because they may increase the risk of more side effects.

Overdose: Symptoms are bloody or black tarry stools, confusion or change in behavior, diarrhea, dizziness or light-headedness, flushing or redness of the face, headaches, increased urination, irritability, loss of appetite, muscle twitching, seizures, stomach cramps or pain, trembling, troubled sleep, unusually fast breathing, pounding or irregular heartbeat, unusual tiredness or weakness, or vomiting blood or material that looks like coffee grounds. These side effects require a doctor's attention as soon as possible.

Proper Use: For this medicine to be quick acting, it is best that you take it with a glass of water on an empty stomach either one hour before meals or two hours after meals. If the medicine upsets your stomach, your doctor may suggest taking it with meals to reduce irritation.

Dosage: This medicine must be taken every day in regularly spaced doses. If you miss a dose, take it as soon as possible. However, if it is almost time for your next dose, skip the missed dose and go back to your regular schedule. Do not double dose. Your doctor should check your progress at regular visits, especially for the first few weeks after you begin taking this medicine. A blood test may be taken to determine whether the dosage should be changed.

Dietary Recommendations: Avoid eating or drinking large amounts of caffeine-containing foods or beverages such as chocolate, cocoa, tea, coffee, and cola drinks because they may add to an excessive stimulation of the central nervous system. Do not eat carbohydrate-rich foods and charcoil-broiled foods regularly because they may make the medicine less effective.

How To Store: Store away from heat and direct light. Do not store the capsule or tablet form in the bathroom medicine cabinet because heat and moisture may cause the medicine to break down. If you store it in the refrigerator, keep from freezing. If the medicine is outdated, flush the capsule, tablet, or liquid form down the toilet.

Cromolyn

Cromolyn (also called cromolyn sodium) is taken by inhalation through the mouth. It is usually used before and during exposure to substances that cause allergic reaction to prevent wheezing or difficulty in breathing. Cromolyn comes in three forms: a powder, which can be taken with a spinhaler (a device that propels the medication into the lungs); a solution, which can be inhaled through a nebulizer machine; or a metered-dose inhaler.

Generic Names: Cromolyn and cromolyn sodium.

Brand Names: Intal and Sodium Cromoglycate.

Effects: Acts on certain cells in the body, called mast cells, to prevent them from releasing substances that cause asthma.

Prescribed For: Prevention of allergic reactions that cause asthma attacks. Used also to prevent attacks caused by exercise. It will not relieve an attack that has already started. If this medicine is used during a severe attack, it may cause irritation and make the attack worse.

What Your Doctor Must Know:

- If you believe you are allergic to cromolyn, had any allergic reaction to other inhalation aerosols, or had any unusual reaction to lactose, milk, or milk products.
- If you are pregnant, planning to become pregnant, or are breast-feeding.
- If you have a history of heart, kidney, or liver disease.

Side Effects: Cromolyn commonly causes a cough or hoarseness in the throat (gargling and rinsing the mouth after each dose may help prevent these effects). Less frequent side effects are sneezing and stuffy nose, irritated throat, or watering of the eyes. These side effects usually do not require medical attention unless they persist.

More Serious Side Effects: In rare instances the drug may cause difficult or painful urination, dizziness, headache, wheezing, joint pain and swelling, muscle pain and weakness, nausea or vomiting, rash, hives or itching, swelling of the eyes and lips, tightness in the chest, troubled breathing, and difficulty in swallowing. On rare occasions you might experience chills, difficulty in breathing, unusual sweating, and perhaps severe wheezing. These side effects require a doctor's attention as soon as possible.

Proper Use: Keep the spray away from the eyes because it may cause irritation. Do not swallow cromolyn capsules used for inhalation.

Dosage: Do not take larger doses or use more often than recommended by your doctor. If your are using the inhaled variety of cromolyn, take it every day in regularly spaced doses. Up to four weeks may pass before you feel the full effects of the medicine. If you miss a dose, take it as soon as possible. Then take any remaining doses for that day at regularly spaced intervals. Do not double dose.

How To Store: Store away from heat. Store the capsule or solution form of this medicine away from direct light. Store the aerosol form away from direct sunlight. Do not store the capsule form in the bathroom medicine cabinet because heat and moisture may cause the medicine to break down. Do not puncture, break, or burn the aerosol container, even if it is empty.

Adrenocorticoids (Inhaled)

Adrenocorticoids belong to the general family of medicines called steroids. The steroids we discuss here are inhaled through the mouth to help prevent asthma attacks. Inhaled steroids don't cause as many side effects as steroids that are swallowed or injected (see page 65). An inhaled steroid is often the first steroid medication used in a routine asthma program because it reaches the site of the blocked bronchial tubes quickly and produces fewer side effects. On occasion your doctor may begin with an inhaled bronchodilator to open the airways, which will allow the steroid to penetrate into the airways more effectively. These drugs will not relieve an asthma attack that has already started. As a preventive medication, inhaled steroids are used to reduce the number and severity of your asthma attacks.

Generic Names: Beclomethasone, dexamethasone, flunisolide, and triamcinolone.

Brand Names: AeroBid, Azmacort, Beclovent, Decadron, Respihaler, and Vanceril.

Effects: Acts on the tissues that line the nasal passages, mouth, trachea and bronchial tubes.

Prescribed For: Control of allergic rhinitis and bronchial asthma and reduces frequency and severity of asthmatic attacks.

What Your Doctor Must Know:

- If you believe you are allergic to adrenocorticoids or aerosol spray inhalation medicines, or preservatives or dyes.
- If you are pregnant, planning to become pregnant, or are breast-feeding.
- If you are using any inhalation adrenocorticoid and have an infection of the mouth, throat, or lungs, or if you have ever had tuberculosis.

- (To take dexamethasone or triamcinolone inhalation aerosol) If you have a bone disease, colitis, diabetes, diverticulitis, fungal infection, glaucoma, heart disease, herpes simplex infection of the eye, high blood pressure, high cholesterol levels, kidney disease or kidney stones, liver disease, myasthenia gravis, stomach ulcer or other stomach problems, or an underactive thyroid.

Side Effects: These drugs can cause mild abdominal pain, a bloated feeling or gas, constipation, diarrhea, dizziness, headache, heartburn or indigestion, loss of appetite, loss of smell or sense of taste, nervousness or restlessness, and an unpleasnat taste in the mouth. Less common is a cough without a sign of an infection; a dry or irritated nose, tongue, or throat; a false sense of well-being; shakiness or faintness; hoarseness or other voice changes; increase in appetite; troubled sleeping; unexplained nosebleeds; and an increase in sweating. These symptoms usually do not require medical attention and may go away during treatment as your body adjusts to the medicine. If they persist, see your doctor.

More Serious Side Effects: Chest pain; chills, fever, and sore throat; creamy white, curdlike patches inside the mouth; increased susceptibility to infection; nausea or vomiting, skin rash or itching; unusually fast or pounding heartbeat. Less common side effects are decreased or blurred vision; difficulty in swallowing; hives; increased blood pressure; increased thirst; mental depression or other mood or mental changes; swelling of the face, feet, or lower legs; and unusual weight gain. Additional side effects that may occur after you have been using this medicine for a long period of time include acne or other skin problems,; back or rib pain; black, tarry, or bloody stools; filling or rounding out of the face (moon face); frequent urination; irregular heartbeat; menstrual problems; muscle weakness, cramps, or pains; stomach pain or severe continuing burning; unusual tiredness; and wounds that will not heal. See your doctor as soon as any of these side effects occur.

Precaution: If your symptoms do not improve within seven days (for dexamethasone) or within three weeks (for beclomethasone or flunisolide), if you develop a nose, sinus, or throat infection, or if your condition gets worse, call your doctor.

Proper Use: In order to be effective, this medicine should be used regularly as ordered by your doctor. Beclomethasone and dexamethasone are used with a special inhaler. If you do not understand the directions, or if you are not sure how to use the inhaler, check with your doctor. (See page 128 for information about the proper use of an inhaler.)

Dosage: Do not take larger doses or use more often than recommended by your doctor. The medicine usually begins to work in about one week, but up to three weeks may pass before you feel its full effect. If you miss a dose of this medicine and remember it within an hour or so, take it right away. However, if you do not remember until later, skip the missed dose and go back to your regular schedule. Do not double dose.

Dietary Recommendations: Steroids tend to increase sodium and water retention, so avoid large amounts of foods rich in sodium, such as anchovies, green olives, dill pickles, sardines, canned soups and vegetables, and processed cheeses.

How To Store: Store the solution form of this medicine away from heat and direct light. Store the aerosol form away from direct sunlight. Do not puncture, break, or burn the aerosol container, even if it is empty.

Adrenocorticoids/Corticotropin

Adrenocorticoids (cortisonelike medicines) belong to the family of steroids. The adrenal glands of the human body produce certain hormones, or chemical messengers, which are necessary to maintain good health. These anti-inflammatory medications are used to provide relief for inflamed areas of the body and as part of the treatment for a number of different diseases, including severe allergies and asthma. Adrenocorticoids/corticotropin are taken by mouth, given by injection, or used rectally. (For steroids that are inhaled, see page 63.)

Many people with asthma view steroids with concern, especially those that are swallowed or injected, because these drugs have such an impressive impact on so many body functions, which explains their potential for producing a variety of unwanted side effects. However, with proper use you need not expect to experience many or any of them. At no time should concern for their side effects influence the decision to use steroids during acute, difficult-to-manage asthma attacks. Not only are steroids very effective in these circumstances, but even in high doses they can be used with little risk of profound or lasting side effects. What is important to understand, then, is that these medicines are safe and effective if they are used as instructed by your doctor.

Generic Names: Betamethasone, corticotropin, cortisone, dexamethasone, hydrocortisone, methylprednisolone, paramethasone, prednisolone, prednisone, and triamcinolone.

Brand Names: There are more than 100 brand names. A complete list of them can be found in the book *Drug Information for the Consumer* (see Chapter 5). Brand names include Amcort, Asthar, Cortisol, Cortone, Dalalone, Depopred, Dexon, Haldrone, Liquid Pred, Medrone, Panasol, Prednisol TBA, Prelestone, Triam, and Trilone.

Effects: Acts on all sites of inflammation and allergic reactions.

Prescribed For: Relief of swelling, redness, heat and pain in cell tissue.

What Your Doctor Must Know:

- If you believe you are allergic to adrenocorticoids or corticotropin, or to pork products.
- If you are pregnant, planning to become pregnant, or are breast-feeding.
- If you have a bone disease, colitis, diabetes mellitus, diverticulitis, fungus infection or any other infection, glaucoma, heart disease, herpes simplex infection of the eye, high blood pressure, high cholesterol levels, kidney disease or kidney stones, liver disease, myasthenia gravis, overactive or underactive thyroid, stomach ulcer or other stomach or intestine problems, or tuberculosis (or a history of).
- If you are using acetaminophen, acetazolamide, amphotericin B, anabolic steroids, male hormones, blood thinners, antidepressants, oral diabetes medicine, medicine for abdominal or stomach spasm or cramps, medicine for overactive thyroid, barbiturates, carbamazepine, dichlorphenamide, heart medicine, diuretics, ephedrine, female hormones, folic acid, griseofulvin, heparin, insulin, medicine for tuberculosis, medicine for inflammation or pain, methazolamide, mexiletine, oral contraceptives, phenytoin, potassium supplements, primidone, rifampin, somatrem, somatropin, thyroid hormones, troleandomycin, valproic acid, large amounts of antacids, or any medicine that contains a large amount of sodium (salt).

Side Effects With Short-Term Use: Despite their reputation for producing a wide variety of unwanted side effects, when these medicines are used for short periods they usually produce few side effects, except in persons who are especially sensitive to steroids, such as the elderly and children. These side effects are a false sense of well-being, increase in appetite and weight gain (in others it may be a loss of appetite), indigestion, nervousness or restlessness, and troubled sleep. Less often, there might be a darkening or lightening of skin color, dizziness or light-headedness, headaches, and an increase in hair growth on the body or face. These effects should go away during treatment as your body adjusts to the medicine. If they persist, see your doctor.

More Serious Side Effects With Short-Term Use: These side effects are decreased or blurred vision; frequent urination; increased thirst; mental depression or mood changes; burning, numbness, pain, or tingling at or near the place of injection; skin rash or hives; redness, swelling, or any other signs of infection at or near the place of injection. Check with your doctor as soon as possible if any of these side effects occur.

Effects With Long-Term Use: The longer the drug is used, the more likely side effects will occur. In addition to the side effects mentioned earlier, with long-term use of steroids you could experience a burning or pain in the stomach or abdominal area; acne or other skin problems; bloody or black and tarry stools; cataracts; decreased or slow growth (in children); filling or rounding out of the face; hip pain; hallucinations; increase in blood pressure; irregular heartbeat; menstrual problems; muscle cramps or pain; muscle weakness; nausea or vomiting; pain in the back, ribs, arms, or legs (osteoporosis); pitting or depression of skin at the place of injection; reddish-purple lines on the arms, face, legs, trunk, or groin; swelling of the feet or lower legs; thin, shiny skin; unusual bruising; unusual tiredness or weakness; unusual weight gain, or wounds that will not heal. Again, if any of these side effects occur, check with your doctor as soon as possible.

Side Effects After You Stop Taking The Drugs: These drugs can produce strong side effects when you stop taking them. The length of time your body takes to readjust will depend in part on how long you were using the drug. For example, if you have taken large doses of this medicine for a year or more, your body may need as much as a year to adjust. However long that period of adjustment is, you may experience abdominal or stomach or back pain, dizziness or fainting, fever, loss of appetite, muscle or joint pain, nausea or vomiting, shortness of breath, unexplained headaches, unusual tiredness or weakness, or unusual weight loss. Check with your doctor immediately if any of these side effects occur.

Precaution: Before you have skin tests or any kind of surgery or emergency treatment, notify the doctor treating you that you are taking these drugs. While being treated with these medicines, and one year following use, do not have any immunizations without your doctor's approval. Avoid anyone who may have had a recent polio vaccine since they could pass the polio virus on to you during this period. If you are a diabetic, note that this medicine may cause your blood sugar levels to rise. If you notice a change in your urine or blood sugar, check with your doctor.

Proper Use: As we discussed earlier, the adrenal glands produce their own steroids, which are necessary to maintain good health. Since these natural steroids are released in the early morning hours, it is best to take oral steroids early in the morning as well. If the steroids were to be taken only at random times during the day, the body may assume that it no longer needs to produce its own steroids, which could develop into a serious problem. This is called adrenal suppression. The body's reliance on the steroids you are taking seriously increases the risk of steroid side effects. Therefore, use this medicine only as directed by your doctor. This means that you are not to use more or less of it, use it more often, or use it for a longer period of time than your doctor instructed. At no time should you stop using the medicine without first checking with your doctor. In fact, your doctor should probably check your progress at regular visits both while you are using the medicine and for a period after you have stopped.

Dosage: It is best to take steroids in the morning. When appropriate, it is even better to take them on alternate mornings because it allows the adrenal glands to continue their production of natural steroids without being affected by the steroid medication. On the other hand, taking steroids in the morning and again later on in the day raises the same problem of adrenal suppression. In some serious cases of asthma, it is necessary to take steroids more than once a day, but the best plan would be to reduce the dosage of steroid medication as soon as possible to once a day or, even better, to every other day.

If you miss a dose of this medicine, follow this procedure:

IF YOU TAKE THE MEDICINE SEVERAL TIMES A DAY, take the missed dose as soon as possible and go back to your regular schedule. If you don't remember until the next day, skip the missed dose and don't double the next one.

IF YOU TAKE THE MEDICINE ONCE A DAY, take the missed

dose as soon as possible. If you don't remember until the next day, skip the missed dose and don't double the next one.

IF YOU TAKE THE MEDICINE EVERY OTHER DAY, take the missed dose as soon as possible, if you remember that morning. If you don't remember until that day, wait and take it the following morning. Then skip a day and start your regular schedule again.

Dietary Recommendations: Restrict your intake of dietary sodium (salt), because these drugs tend to increase your sodium and water retention. Extended use of steroids can create a loss of calcium and potassium. Therefore, your doctor may advise you to increase your consumption of potassium- and calcium-rich foods and take a daily supplement of 400 to 800 International Units of vitamin D. Again, with long-term use, steroids can contribute to the breakdown of body protein. Your doctor may recommend a diet rich in protein such as fish, beans, peas, and soy products. Meats may be a rich source of protein, but their fats could contribute to an undesirable weight gain. To reduce the chances of stomach distress, take this medicine with milk or with meals. To avoid the excessive thirst many people experience with these drugs, drink eight glasses of fluid per day. However, you shouldn't drink alcohol while taking this medicine unless you have checked with your doctor.

How To Store: Store away from heat and direct light. Do not store the tablet forms in the bathroom medicine cabinet because heat and moisture may cause the medicine to break down. Store the liquid forms of this medicine in the refrigerator, but keep from freezing. If the medicine is outdated, flush it down the toilet.

Antihistamines

Antihistamines are used to relieve or prevent symptoms of hay fever and other types of allergies. Antihistamines, which work to block the release from mast cells of a chemical called histamine, do not open the airways or relieve asthma symptoms, even though histamine is one of the chemicals that cause asthma symptoms. Instead, these medicines bring under control other symptoms caused by histamine, such as nasal itchiness, sneezing, and a runny nose.

Treating these upper respiratory tract symptoms with antihistamines is a cause for concern for some people with asthma because they fear that the medicine will irritate the sinuses and throat by making them too dry. A more serious concern is that the antihistamine may dry the airways. However, an experienced patient usually learns when and how much of an antihistamine to use. It is best to begin use of this medicine, and all others for that matter, under the supervision of your doctor.

Some antihistamine preparations are available only with your doctor's prescription. Others are available without a prescription.

Generic Names: Azatadine, bromodiphenhydramine (available in cough/cold combination products), brompheniramine, carbinoxamine, chlorpheniramine, clemastine, cyproheptadine, dexchlorpheniramine, dimenhydrinate, diphenhydramine, dephenylpyraline, doxylamine, phenindamine, pyrilamine, terfenadine, tripelennamine, and triprolidine.

Brand Names: There are more than 100 brands available in the United States, including Alka-Seltzer Plus Cold Medicine, Allerest, Benadryl, Chlor-Trimeton, Clistin, Contac, CoTylenol, Decapryn, Dimetane, Diafen, Dristan, Nolahist, Optimine, Periactin, Polaramine, Seldane, Sinarest, Sine-Off, Sinutab, Sudafed, Triaminic, and Teldrin.

Effects: Acts on those tissues that release excessive histamine as part of an allergic reaction.

Prescribed For: Relief of symptoms associated with allergic rhinitis and allergic reactions in the skin.

What Your Doctor Must Know:

- If you believe you are allergic to antihistamines, or to foods, sulfites or other preservatives, or dyes.
- If you are pregnant, planning to be pregnant, or are breast-feeding. (Small amounts of antihistamines can pass into the breast milk and cause some side effects such as unusual excitement or irritability in the infant.)
- If you are on a low-salt or any other special diet.
- If you have an enlarged prostate, glaucoma, urinary tract blockage, difficult urination, and, of course, if you have asthma.
- If you are taking amantadine, medicine for abdominal or stomach spasm or cramps, aspirin or other salicylates, cisplatin, clonidine, guanabenz, haloperidol, ipratropium, maprotiline, methyldopa, metyrosine, paromomycin, phenothiazines, procainamide, trazodone, tricyclic antidepressants, vancomycin, any monoamine oxidase (MAO) inhibitors, or any central nervous system depressants (antihistamines will add to the effects of any medicine—this includes alcohol—that slows down the nervous system, causing excessive drowsiness).

Side Effects: With the exception of terfenadine, antihistamines frequently cause drowsiness and a thickening of any bronchial secretions. Less common is blurred vision or a change in vision; confusion; difficult or painful urination; dizziness; dryness of the mouth, nose, or throat; increased sensitivity of the skin to the sun; loss of appetite; nightmares; ringing or buzzing sound in the ears; skin rash; stomach upset or pain; unusual excitement, nervousness, restlessness, or irritability; unusual increase in sweating; or unusually fast heartbeat. Children and the elderly are usually more sensitive to the effects of antihistamines. Otherwise, these side effects may go away during treatment as your body adjusts to the medicine. If not, check with your doctor.

Overdose: In addition to any of the previous symptoms that persist or are severe, signs such as unusual bleeding or bruising, unsteadiness, faintness, redness of the face, hallucinations, seizures, shortness of breath, or trouble sleeping would suggest that you are taking too much of the antihistamines. When these effects occur, check with your doctor.

Precaution: Do not take any medicine that depresses the central nervous system, such as sedatives, tranquilizers, sleeping medicine, prescription pain medicine or narcotics, barbiturates, medicine for seizures, muscle relaxants, or anesthetics, including some dental anesthetics. Because drowsiness may occur, know what your reaction is to antihistamines before you drive, use a machine, or do other jobs that require you to be alert.

Proper Use: If you take this drug on a regular basis and you miss a dose, take it as soon as possible. However, if it is almost time for your next dose, skip the missed dose and go back to your regular schedule.

Dosage: Take antihistamines as directed. Do not take larger doses or use more often than recommended by your doctor. If your asthma symptoms grow worse or cause you to be constantly sleepy, stop using them and check with your doctor.

Dietary Recommendations: It is recommended that you take the tablet form of the drug with food or a glass of milk to reduce the possibility of any stomach irritation. If the tablet is a time-release or extended-release, swallow it whole.

How To Store: Store this medicine away from heat and direct light. Don't store the tablet form in the bathroom, as the heat or moisture may cause the drug to break down.

Ipratropium

Ipratropium, also called ipratropium bromide, belongs to the group of medicines called bronchodilators. It is a new drug that is inhaled to control the symptoms of asthma by preventing the actions of the nervous system on airway muscle cells and thereby opening up the airways of the lungs. It is also used to reduce mucus secretion. Its characteristic is that it opens the airways slowly but with effects lasting up to four hours.

Generic Name: Ipratropium, and ipratropium bromide.
Brand Name: Atrovent.
Effects: Acts to open up the bronchial tubes or air passages of the lung.
Prescribed For: Relief of difficult breathing associated with acute attacks of asthma.
What Your Doctor Must Know:

- If you believe you are allergic to atropine, belladonna, hyoscyamine, scopolamine, or to other inhaled aerosol medicines.
- If you are pregnant, planning to become pregnant, or are breast-feeding.
- If you have difficult urination, an enlarged prostate, or glaucoma.
- If you are taking amantadine, antihistamines, medicine for abdominal or stomach spasms or cramps, buclizine, chlorprothixene, cyclizine, cyclobenzaprine, dicyclomine, disopyramide, flavoxate, haloperidol, loxapine, maprotiline, meclizine, methylphenidate, orphenadrine, oxybutynin, phenothiazines, pimozide, procainamide, quinidine, thiothixene, trazodone, medicine in the eye, or other oral inhaled aerosols for asthma or breathing problems.

Side Effects: This drug may cause a dryness of the mouth or throat and a headache. Less common is a bad taste in the mouth, blurred vision, difficult urination, dizziness, nausea, stuffy nose, trembling, or an unusual pounding heartbeat. These side effects usually go away once the body adjusts to the medicine. However, if they persist, check with your doctor.
Overdose: If these side effects become severe and continue, it may indicate that you are absorbing too much of the drug. Other signs of

excess absorption are unsteadiness, confusion, fever, hallucinations, skin rash, slurred speech, unusual drowsiness or weakness, unusual excitement, irritability or nervousness, unusual warmth, dryness, or redness of the face.

Precaution: Keep the spray away from your eyes because it may cause irritation.

Proper Use: Using two or more inhaled aerosol medicines together can increase the risk of side effects. If you are using another broncho-dilator in an inhaled aerosol form, use it first. Then wait about five minutes before using the ipratropium. However, if you are using an adrenocorticoid inhaled aerosol or cromolyn inhaled aerosol, use the ipratropium first. Then wait about five minutes before using the other inhaled aerosol. If you are taking more than one inhalation for each dose, allow one minute between the inhalations to ensure maximum benefit of the drug.

Dosage: Take ipratropium as directed. Do not take larger doses or use more often than recommended by your doctor. If you miss a dose, take it as soon as possible. However, if it is almost time for your next dose, skip the missed dose and go back to your regular schedule. Do not double dose. If your breathing problems do not clear up, or if they grow worse, check with your doctor.

How To Store: Store away from heat and direct sunlight. If you store in the refrigerator, keep from freezing. Do not puncture, break, or burn the container, even if it is empty. Dispose of the medicine once it is outdated.

Pseudoephedrine

Pseudoephedrine is a decongestant and is used in the treatment of asthma because it provides relief of nasal or sinus congestion caused by cold, sinusitis, or hay fever. As mentioned previously, any treatment of the upper respiratory system also helps to reduce asthma symptoms or the likelihood of their occurrence. Decongestants do this by reducing nasal stuffiness, which helps remove some of the pressure in the sinuses.

There are many decongestants that can be used. With pseudoephedrine, some preparations are available only with a prescription, while other preparations, called "over-the-counter" drugs, can be purchased in a drugstore without a prescription.

Generic Name: Pseudoephedrine.

Brand Names: Afrinol Repetabs, Cenafed, Children's Sudafed Liquid, Decofed, Dorcol Pediatric Formula, Halofed, Neofed, Neo-Synephrinol Day Relief, Novafed, PediaCare, Peedee Dose Decongestant, Sinufed, Sudafed, Sudafed S.A., Sudagest, and Sudrin.

Effects: Acts on the small blood vessels in the lining of the nose, sinuses and the throat.

Prescribed For: Relief of congestion of the nose, sinuses and throat associated with allergic disorder and infections.

What Your Doctor Must Know:

- If you are allergic to albuterol, amphetamines, ephedrine, epinephrine, isoproterenol, metaproterenol, norepinephrine, phenylephrine, phenylpropanolamine, or terbutaline; or if you are allergic to foods, sulfites or other preservatives, or dyes.
- If you are pregnant, planning to become pregnant, or are breast-feeding.
- If you are taking amantadine, amphetamines, medicine for high blood pressure, diet pills, beta-blockers, caffeine, chlophedianol, heart medicine, diuretics, levodopa, medicine for asthma or other breathing problems, methylphenidate, medicine for angina, medicine for colds, sinus problems, or hay fever (this includes nose drops and sprays), pemoline, thyroid hormones, or monoamine oxidase (MAO) inhibitors within the past two weeks.

Side Effects: These drugs may cause nervousness, restlessness, and troubled sleep. Less common is difficult or painful urination, dizziness or light-headedness, headache, nausea or vomiting, trembling, troubled breathing, unusual increase in sweating, unusually fast or pounding heartbeat, unusual paleness, or weakness. These side effects usually do not require medical attention and should go away as your body adjusts to the medicine. However, if they persist, see your doctor.

Overdose: Symptoms are hallucinations, increase in blood pressure, irregular heartbeat, seizures, severe or constant shortness of breath or troubled breathing, unusually fast breathing, severe or constantly slow or fast heartbeat, unusual and exaggerated nervousness, restlessness, or excitement. See your doctor as soon as possible if these side effects occur.

Proper Use: If you are taking an extended-release capsule form of this medicine, swallow the capsule whole. If the capsule is too large to swallow, mix the contents of the capsule with jam or jelly and swallow without chewing. If it is in tablet form, swallow the tablet whole. Do not crush, break, or chew before swallowing. If you have trouble sleeping, take the last daily dose of this medicine a few hours before going to bed.

Dosage: If you miss a dose of this medicine and you remember within an hour or so of the missed dose, take it right away. However, if you do not remember until later, skip the missed dose and go back to your regular schedule. Do not double dose.

How To Store: Store away from heat and direct light. Do not store the capsule or tablet form in the bathroom medicine cabinet because moisture and heat may cause the medicine to break down. If you store the liquid form in the refrigerator, keep from freezing. Dispose of any outdated medicine by flushing the contents of the container down the toilet, unless otherwise directed.

Children and Asthma

Asthma is one of the most common diseases in children. Nearly one-third of the approximately nine million to fifteen million people with asthma in the United States are under the age of seventeen. The impact of asthma on the lives of many children and their families is significant—asthma is responsible for 25 percent of all school absences, and it is estimated that each year asthma results in more than twelve million days spent in bed rest and more than twenty-five million days of restricted activity.

Asthma is, for children and adults, a controversial disease because there are considerable differences of opinion about the relative importance of various causes of asthma symptoms and the relative merit of various treatments. Furthermore, it's a disease whose course is very difficult to predict in any given child, and there is no way of predicting whether any one child will continue to have asthma symptoms when he or she becomes an adult. However, statistics suggest that asthma symptoms are more likely to continue into adulthood if (1) the child is a boy, (2) the child has developed asthma before the age of two, (3) allergies have contributed to the problem, and (4) the wheezing was not successfully managed by the doctor.

It is estimated that about half of all children who develop asthma will outgrow the illness by the time they reach their teenage years. Even though laboratory tests may show traces of abnormal lung function, such children will no longer be burdened by any of the overt symptoms, such as wheezing and coughing, that had been a part of their asthma episodes. In many cases the child will show a complete recovery from the asthma by the age of six. One explanation for this development is that the child's airways have grown larger and wider, making air flow easier. It should be noted that many children who seemingly outgrow their asthma symptoms develop allergy-related diseases, such as hay fever, as adults.

Much of what was discussed earlier about treatment of asthma for adults applies to children as well. However, there are differences, too.

Most children who have a mild form of asthma can be successfully treated at home and in the doctor's office. With prompt treatment and cooperation by the child and his or her parents, most asthma episodes consisting of a mild cough, nasal discharge, slight wheeze, or mild temperature will soon subside. But for those children with severe symptoms, asthma can be a formidable disease that sometimes results in multiple visits to the hospital emergency room and hospitalizations. The symptoms in these cases may range from rapid breathing and increased heart rate to heavy perspiration and a clearly audible wheeze. Usually the child is extremely anxious and can become hysterical in his or her struggle to breathe. These children and their parents suffer through some frightening moments, especially when breathing becomes very difficult. With proper treatment, however, most cases of very severe asthma can be controlled. It may be a small comfort to parents with a child who is suffering acutely from asthma symptoms to know that fatalities due to asthma are still very rare among children.

Causes

As with adult asthma, childhood asthma results from a highly sensitive response of the airways to various stimuli, such as allergens, pollutants, emotional problems, exposure to cold weather, too much exercise, and infections.

Most upper respiratory tract infections among infants are caused by viruses rather than bacteria. These infections are often mistaken as a sign of asthma. The most common respiratory virus, called the respiratory syncytial virus, causes an inflammation of the bronchioles. This condition as well as other respiratory infections can look initially very much like asthma, causing the child to wheeze, cough, breathe rapidly, and develop a fever. Croup is another viral infection that mimics asthma because its symptoms include nighttime cough and difficulties in breathing. What is important to understand is that the cough is usually in the throat and not in the lungs. Also, when croup becomes more serious, it generally makes it difficult for the child to breath in, whereas difficulty in breathing out is more indicative of asthma. Then again, when the wheezing, coughing, or troubled breathing continue, asthma is frequently suspected. Other viruses that can cause wheezing and often develop into asthma are those associated with infections of the upper respiratory tract, including the common cold.

Flu (influenza) is thought to be another culprit of bronchial spasms, so it's wise to consider a flu vaccination. If your child is taking theophylline, make sure your doctor knows your plans to get a flu vaccination, since the vaccination can sometimes alter the effectiveness of the drug.

IRRITANTS: Although the mechanism by which air pollution triggers asthma is relatively unknown, the irritating effect on the bronchi of some pollutants is no mystery. For example, the risk of asthma and other childhood respiratory diseases is significantly increased when the child is exposed to cigarette smoke. Exposure to this major lung pollutant not only enhances the likelihood and frequency of asthma episodes, but it can cause the attacks to be all the more severe. Aerosol sprays, perfumes, and strong odors of almost any type may also serve as irritants for the child with asthma. Therefore, it's advised that you use with great care pungent cleaning agents, room fresheners, perfumes, and the like around the child with asthma.

The complete list of potential irritants is too vast to be included here. Let it be said that it's critical that through close and attentive observation parents learn what substances and conditions are responsible for asthma attacks in their child. For example, some children with asthma have been known to have flareups due to cold foods or drinks, while others have had asthma symptoms triggered by quite normal hormonal changes during their puberty years.

Usually children with asthma, as well as adults, have more than one factor that triggers the asthma attack. In addition, these factors may change over time. A child may have trouble with respiratory infections as a toddler, wheeze when he or she exercises as a young child, and suffer from asthma triggered by pollen allergy as a teenager. The common bond among all these changing factors that cause asthma symptoms is the child's inherited defect in the lungs. That never goes away.

ALLERGIES: As we learned in Chapter 1, an allergy is an abnormal reaction to various substances in the environment that occurs when a person with an inherited tendency to allergy is exposed to them. An allergic response can show itself in a variety of different ways depending on the individual. The response can range from sneezing and itching episodes to skin rashes and headaches.

EMOTIONAL PROBLEMS: The relative significance of emotional problems in triggering asthma episodes in children is one of the controversies surrounding the cause and treatment of this disease. In the minds of some people a dispute or confusion exists as to whether psychological difficulties in a child can develop into asthma. Some people hold to the belief that emotional problems can only trigger an asthma episode if the child has the inherited disposition for the disease and only after the illness has developed due to other causes or triggers. Even there, the issue of whether emotional problems can ever actually trigger an attack of asthma is widely disputed. At a minimum, it can be said that no amount of emotional stress can actually cause asthma unless someone already has abnormally irritable bronchial tubes. Therefore, asthma is not a psychosomatic disease.

Whatever is to be said about the controversy, there is substantial evidence that emotions do play a role in many cases of asthma. As to what extent, it is not easily determined. Just the fact, however, that children with asthma appear more frequently in the emergency rooms of hospitals on Friday and Saturday nights suggests that their attacks are related to their home life. It's also possible that some children use the asthma to manipulate their family or doctor. To get out of going to school, to avoid some punishment, or to get attention, children have been known to skip their medications or work themselves into such an emotional state that an asthma episode seems to develop. Nonetheless, asthma must be considered a physical disease, though one that can be worsened by emotional stress.

EXERCISE: Even though it is a common trigger for asthma attacks in children, exercise should not be avoided. On the contrary, exercise should be encouraged in all children. It permits the child with asthma to play with other children and not feel painfully different. Besides building fitness, exercise builds self-esteem and confidence.

Before exercise will trigger an asthma attack, it usually must be vigorous or last a minimum of five to ten minutes. Even then the child may not necessarily wheeze, but he or she may tire more easily than fellow playmates. If exercise continues to trigger symptoms, the child needs to learn when changes occur in breathing patterns that would indicate possible trouble. If the child begins to wheeze or cough, he or she should take a short rest. It may be necessary for the child to learn to pace himself or herself so as not to get too tired and risk a flareup.

The child should learn to use an inhaler (see page 128) to relieve any early chest tightening (bronchospasm), or better yet as a pretreatment before vigorous exercise. At least 80 percent of exercise-induced asthma can be prevented by using cromolyn or an inhaled bronchodilator before exercising. In short, with proper education most children can learn to exercise without fear of asthma attacks.

MEDICATIONS: Some medications do play a part in inducing an asthma episode. (See "Medication," page 46.) In some cases, aspirin has triggered episodes. The child with asthma who has demonstrated a sensitivity to aspirin should be given an aspirin substitute. Acetaminophen (Tylenol is one brand) is an acceptable alternative.

Effects of Asthma in Children

Many parents have an understandable concern that their child is in peril of becoming a cripple because of his or her asthma. However, it is only in rare cases that a child suffers an asthma-related impairment that could be considered crippling.

In cases in which a child is at risk of long-term physical effects due to asthma, generally the disease has been unusually severe and unmanageable over a number of years. The fact is that with the help of an effective treatment program, the vast majority of children with asthma outgrow the disease to lead perfectly normal lives. As with most health care problems, the sooner the asthma is brought under control, the less likely any of the following effects will occur—let alone become permanent.

PHYSICAL EFFECTS: In most cases, the physical damage of the asthma can be reversed. However, the longer the asthma has been poorly controlled, the greater the risk that some of the damage might become permanent.

Lungs: A major area of parental concern is the child's lungs. Many parents believe that the constant tightening of the bronchial muscles, swelling of the mucosa, or formation of mucus plugs places the child at risk of developing scar tissue. The fact is that there appears to be no scarring or any other permanent damage to the lungs due directly to asthma.

Heart: The child's heart is another concern of parents. Again, even though children with asthma develop rapid heart rates due to anxiety, medications, or labored breathing, no permanent damage should occur. A child's heart is capable of handling the extra load. However, severe asthma that causes persistently low levels of oxygen in the blood can adversely affect the heart. This is one reason why it is critical to get severe asthma and acute asthma attacks under control immediately.

Posture: If the child has difficulty breathing normally, he or she may develop poor posture. The struggle to breathe in and out may have required the child to habitually use the shoulder and chest muscles. As a result, he or she may carry the shoulders up and forward, creating a round-shouldered look.

Growth: Mild or moderate asthma never affects the growth of a child. However, children who have had severe asthma for years grow more slowly than children without asthma, and often their full growth potential is never achieved. One of the side effects of steroids, a medication used in the treatment of severe cases of asthma, is growth retardation in children. (See "Adrenocorticoids," page 65.) When these drugs are used prudently and only over a short period, it's believed that the growth of young children usually resumes when steroids are stopped.

Exercise: Most children with long-term asthma probably don't exercise enough. Children with persistent breathing problems are hard at work taking air in and getting rid of it. These children frequently complain of being tired or "run down." If their asthma is always triggered by exercise, they will restrict their activity levels more and more, with the result that they become poorly conditioned and even less able to exercise without fatigue.

PSYCHOLOGICAL EFFECTS: Clearly not all children with asthma develop serious emotional problems. Some will have few or no problems. But for those children who suffer from recurring asthma during their formative years, psychological problems may become a health issue.

Self-Esteem: A child who sees that he or she is unable to compete in school activities, is absent from school more than anyone else, and falls behind in his or her schoolwork as a result is bound to feel different—perhaps inferior. Feeling a burden to his or her family reinforces the notion that he or she is different. This attitude can lead to a loss of self-esteem and depression. (See "Family Concerns," page 121.)

Anger and Guilt: A not uncommon feeling for the young child with severe asthma is anger and resentment that he or she should be burdened with a persistent problem while others are not. "Why me?" is a frequent complaint. The disruption in the home caused by asthma may magnify other family problems for which the child feels he or she is being unfairly blamed or for which he or she mistakenly accepts responsibility.

Fear and Depression: Some children may fear that they will not grow up to be physically "normal"; if the asthma is very severe, they may develop a fear of their own death, although they may not speak about it or understand it as such. For a child with a history of severe asthma, depression may be a sign of these fears.

Treatment

Asthma cannot be cured, but it can be managed. The goal of asthma management is to allow the child to live as normal a life as possible using these three strategies for preventing asthma flareups: (1) avoiding known allergens and irritants; (2) maintaining a program of effective medication; and (3) where appropriate, following a prudent program of allergy immunotherapy (shots).

AVOIDANCE TECHNIQUES: One of the most important features of a child's treatment is a caring and knowledgeable family. Parents should be as fully informed as possible about the disease and specifically the known or suspected causes of the disease in their child. As we mentioned in Chapter 1, there are several kinds of allergens, such as mites, animal hair, and molds, that can be found in and inhaled from common house dust. Other allergens are pollens, foods, substances that make contact with the skin, and substances that are injected. Careful attention must be paid when it comes to understanding the physical environment in which the child lives.

Perhaps the most likely manner in which the child will come in contact with an offending allergen or irritant is through breathing. Air quality is important for everyone, but it is especially important for the child with asthma. What is acceptable air quality for everyone else may be "bad" for the adult or child with asthma, simply because the air contains a substance or quality that triggers asthma symptoms. In many cases, it's not easy to discover what's in the air that's causing the problem.

As a result, parents of children with asthma must be especially aware of where potential threats to their child's health exist. This awareness starts with noting when coughing or wheezing begins. If the child seems to wheeze slightly whenever he or she is in the basement, you may assume that molds are at fault unless, of course, you learn that paints and cleaners are stored there as well. If the child wakes each morning with a ten-minute cough, he or she could be allergic to feathers in the pillow, or animal hair from the household pet, or dust from the bookshelves. As you can see, trying to learn initially what sets off asthma symptoms in a child is not always easy, since asthma symptoms are almost never the result of just one or two substances.

Knowing in advance what causes the asthma symptoms is the most basic element of any prevention program. Many parents have found that keeping a journal is helpful since the aggregate total of weeks or months of data gathering can offer a clearer and more detailed picture of the likely triggers of the asthma. (See "Keeping a Record," page 119.) If you rely solely on your memory, you may overlook one or more circumstances that could be the cause of an asthma symptom. Many asthma flareups occur several hours after exposure to the offending irritant.

Once you learn what is causing the problem, the decision comes down to how the asthma patient will avoid the offending substance or circumstance. This decision is not necessarily easy or practical.

Allergyproofing the House: The infinite number of tiny particles of house dust inhaled every day potentially can irritate the lungs to produce an asthma episode. Therefore, it's genuinely worthwhile to reduce the amount of dust in the home of a child with asthma. Tackling the problems of dustproofing your house is not quite as overwhelming as it first appears. Once the initial changes are instituted, you will be surprised how dust can be reasonably managed. Earlier we talked about how your doctor may ask a number of questions about your house in an effort to locate sources of irritants or allergens. You can use that same list for your own check (see page 40).

The Bedroom: Because a child spends probably eight to ten hours each day in the bedroom, that room needs to be dustproofed more thoroughly than any other in the house.

The following are some guidelines. To begin with, if it's washable, it's probably okay. For example, washable children's stuffed animals, bedspreads, and draperies are acceptable. On the other hand, venetian blinds are not recommended because they collect dust and usually are not easily cleaned. The bedroom should be thoroughly and completely cleaned once a week, including mopping the entire surface of the floors and walls. If the item cannot be washed, then it must be cleaned in a manner that removes the dust that it inevitably traps during the periods between cleanings. What cannot be cleaned thoroughly, such as some stuffed teddy bears, should be removed.

Books: Books not only collect dust, but they're ideal for the growth of mold. The best way to deal with books, which can never be dust free, is to remove them from the child's bedroom.

Pillows: Pillows should be synthetic, machine washable, and thoroughly dried. Feathers are unacceptable because they cannot be washed and they contain animal allergens of their own. Even foam rubber pillows are a concern because, if not replaced every few years, they can support the growth of molds. Just because an item can be washed does not mean it is necessarily acceptable. For example, cotton, a plant fiber which can be cleaned easily, is acceptable; wool, which can be cleaned but is an animal fiber, is not acceptable.

Mattress: Since a mattress is a prime location for the growth of dust mites, a cover or casing made of plastic or vinyl, with zippers, is required to seal the mattress tightly. If you prefer a comfortable mattress pad under the bed sheets, make it a washable one.

Position of the Bed: The bed should be placed out of direct line of the air vent as dust enters the room through the heating and cooling systems. One bed should not be stacked on top of another in the manner of bunk beds because the bottom bed is subject to dust falling from the one above.

Furniture: Heavily upholstered, overstuffed furniture can collect almost more dust than any other piece of furniture in the house. If you must have one in the house, don't place it in the bedroom. It may lose some of its appeal, but if the child likes to sit in the chair, cover the chair with a vinyl or plastic cover.

Closets: The closet in the bedroom may be out of sight but it also hoards dust that can be released into the air of the bedroom. Avoid using it as a storage area, and when you clean the room, clean the closet.

Pets: It may be obvious, but pets should not sleep in the same room as the child and, if possible, pets should not have access to the room. The best place for a pet to be kept is outdoors.

Allergyproofing the Rest of the House: The advice offered on dustproofing your bedroom applies to the rest of the house. In other words, everything that can be cleaned should be cleaned frequently.

Heating Systems: Furnaces and cooling systems are designed to trap dust and dirt. As a result, their filters must be cleaned or changed frequently. If you have not used the heating or cooling system for a long period, clean or vacuum the registers thoroughly before using them; otherwise you may blow months of accumulated dust throughout the house.

Another measure of precaution is to seal off the bedroom from the rest of the house. A separate heater or air conditioning unit for the bedroom will allow you to control the dust that might enter the room, keeping it far cleaner and with less work.

Carpeting: In the room of a child with allergic asthma, do not use carpeting.

Plants: Overlooked dust collectors in many homes are plants, particularly broad-leafed plants. Frequent dusting not only keeps dust down but keeps plants healthier. If the plant needs to be kept wet all the time, try adding a mold-inhibiting solution to the water. Needless to say, keep plants out of the patient's bedroom.

Odors: Many home products can add irritants to the air and cause problems for the child with asthma or allergies. For example, not only is tobacco smoke a threat, but the smell of tobacco can disturb some people. Although you may not be able to wear special clothes just for smoking—smoking jackets are no longer fashionable or practical—at least be aware that the odor can be troubling. Heavy perfumes and deodorant sprays, along with any other aerosol sprays for the home, are to be avoided. Whenever possible, paints, paint cleaners, and other odoriferous products should be stored in the garage or at least outside of the house proper.

Molds: As we saw earlier, molds or mildew can trigger asthma symptoms. Molds will thrive where there is moisture and high humidity. The two rooms in the house that fit that description are the bathroom and the basement.

The best way to remove molds from the bathroom is to clean the floor and tiles thoroughly with a fungicide. In addition to the areas around the bathroom fixtures that gather moisture, shower curtains are notorious for growing molds.

In the basement, you want to control the level of moisture in the air with proper ventilation or the use of a dehumidifier. It is very important that concrete or cinderblock basement walls are made as waterproof as possible with appropriate repairs and use of appropriate paints. Some people recommend that you add 3 ounces of Dianol (available from a paint store) or 1 ounce of Impregon (available from a drugstore) to each gallon of paint.

Where there is sufficient moisture, molds can grow, virtually anywhere and on virtually anything. Molds or mildew are common in the household and can be recognized in the refrigerator, among other places, on spoiled fruit or old cheese. It is wise to keep refrigerators clean and to throw out any spoiled food. Keep closets well ventilated. Finally, check humidifiers and vaporizers, because they can grow mold like greenhouses.

MEDICATION: In this section we briefly discuss a few items that pertain to children and asthma medications. By no means is this section intended to be complete or comprehensive. For a more extensive discussion of asthma medications, turn to pages 46–75.

For adults and children alike, no asthma medication or combination of medications provides a cure. Medications only control the symptoms, and then only as long as they are properly taken. There's no drug that is effective for every kind of asthma or for every kind of child. For the drug therapy to be effective, it has to be tailored to meet the needs of the individual child. If the first drug the doctor prescribes is not effective, he or she will try others until the right drug or combination of drugs is found to be effective. Even then the drug may have to be changed sometime in the future because the severity of the asthma can change and the child's own growth and development can affect his or her response to the medication. Therefore, to ensure that a specific drug therapy is doing the job it's designed to do, the patient must be reexamined periodically and, at times, the medication adjusted if it's producing any new unwanted side effects.

The following section identifies the six basic categories of drugs for the treatment of asthma as they affect children. Again, for a more detailed look at asthma medications, see pages 46–75.

Theophylline: This is the most widely used drug for the treatment of asthma because it is the most effective. It doesn't appear to lose its effectiveness with long-term use, nor does it have serious long-term side effects (see pages 55–61). As with most drugs, theophylline can produce some side effects if the dosage is too high or when it is first used. In these instances, the child may complain of a sore stomach, a loss of appetite, or a stomachache. He or she also may have a headache or may become dizzy and irritable. When these side effects occur, inform your doctor. In most children, the effect of the theophylline lasts four to eight hours, so the drug may have to be taken several times a day for control of persistent asthma. Some preparations of theophylline—such as elixophyllin and Quibron liquids—have a high alcohol content, and young children may experience troubling side effects from the alcohol.

Bronchodilators: These drugs are used to relieve tightening of the bronchial muscles, as part of a pretreatment program prior to vigorous exercise, or to reverse a wheezing episode (see pages 52–55). The drug is usually administered as an aerosol, or, in severe cases, in a nebulized form through a metered-dose inhaler. (See "Products for Home Use," page 124.) However, most small children don't get the maximum benefit from an inhaler because of poor coordination. Since they are often emotionally upset at the time they need to be medicated, the children can't coordinate the release of the medication with their inhalation. As a result, these children are given devices that reduce coordination problems. (See "Bubble Reservoir" and "Tube," pages 129 and 130.) As a precaution, children should be closely monitored as inhalers can be overused, creating a potentially dangerous situation.

Cromolyn: Cromolyn, which stabilizes the mast cells and prevents allergic reactions in the lungs, comes in different forms—powder, liquid, and metered-dose inhaler (see page 61). Cromolyn can cause an irritated throat and coughing. It is recommended that the powder form not be used when the child is coughing since it may make the condition worse. For the child with allergies, cromolyn is available in special preparations for the nose and eye which may help in preventing hay fever and conjunctivitis (an eye infection).

Steroids: Steroids are the most effective of the asthma medications, but they have the most dangerous side effects. Most of the side effects, however, are not thought to be permanent. The following side effects of long-term use of steroids are of particular concern for children:

- Weight gain. (Steroids usually stimulate appetite.)
- Increased fat deposits in the face and trunk, giving a round-face look to the child.

- Retardation of growth. (NOTE: Growth problems in children with severe asthma are due more often to the effect of the asthma on the child rather than the effect of the steroid that may have been used in the treatment.)
- Suppression of the natural production of steroids by the adrenal glands. If steroids are given over a long period of time, the child may have difficulty producing enough steroids for stressful situations. Therefore, steroid medication is usually reduced gradually after a long treatment period.

Inhaled Steroids: These steroids differ from those taken by mouth in that they don't require as high a dosage and they don't affect the entire body. Their disadvantage is that they are difficult to use for small children and are not effective in a severe attack of asthma.

Antihistamines: Antihistamines are used to treat some allergic symptoms (see page 69). The controversy surrounding their use by asthma patients is that the drying effect produced by antihistamines may worsen the asthma condition. Recent studies indicate that newer antihistamines, such as astemizole and terfenadine, may be helpful for allergy-related asthma conditions. If antihistamines are used to treat the child with asthma, they should be closely monitored so that the child's condition is not adversely affected.

OTHER TREATMENTS: As each child with asthma presents a unique combination of problems, so each one requires a special treatment program to answer the needs posed by those problems. In addition to an individualized program of drug therapy, many children require other treatments to meet the complex needs of their asthmatic condition.

Allergy Injections: There is no broad consensus on the value of allergy shots for children or adults. Before deciding on this kind of therapy for your child, consider the following:

- Results may not be appreciated for at least six months or a year; the program could last three or more years.
- This type of treatment is recommended only for the child who has asthma triggered by allergens that can't be avoided. At the same time, it's not used for asthma problems associated with exercise, climate, or infections. Skin tests are not definitive in identifying the offending allergen. Personal observation is far more reliable.

- Many children are not helped by this type of therapy. If asthma attacks persist following an adequate period of treatment, therapy should be stopped.

Sinus Care: Many children with asthma suffer from chronic sinusitis, an inflammation of the lining of the sinuses (see page 26). The inflammation produces excess mucus which drains from the nose and sinuses. The resultant postnasal drip can irritate the throat, cause coughing, and lead to asthma. A small room vaporizer may reduce some of the symptoms, as can performing a nasal douche before going to bed. The easiest way to douche (wash) the nose is to irrigate the child's nose with a saline (salt) solution administered through an ear-bulb syringe. (Before attempting a nasal douche for the first time, discuss the procedure with the doctor.) Consequently, it's important that the child's nose remain clean. Whenever possible, disposable tissues should be used when blowing the nose because they reduce the possibility of spreading any infection. If the sinusitis persists, you may want to ask your doctor about nasal irrigation to reduce the drainage into the lungs.

Antibiotics: Antibiotics are seldom effective in the treatment of uncomplicated asthma since most bronchial infections are viral in nature and antibiotics are useful only for curbing bacterial infections. If an antibiotic is required, avoid the use of tetracycline because it may permanently discolor the teeth of young children.

Diet and Asthma: There is no dietary regimen that has been proven to be beneficial for children with asthma aside from avoidance of specific foods which have been clearly shown to trigger asthma symptoms. Many parents are eager to supplement their children's diet with vitamins and minerals almost as soon as they fall ill. However, there is no evidence that a therapy of vitamin and mineral supplementation can help children with asthma. Since some proponents of supplementation accept evidence that Vitamin A aids the general health of the lungs, Vitamin E guards against air pollutants, and B complex vitamins play some role in the health of the nervous system, they falsely conclude that these vitamins will help the individual with asthma. There is no evidence at all to support this thinking. Extra vitamins, over and above normal daily requirement, are not necessary, nor are they recommended. (For more information about the problems of children and asthma, see pages 121–123.)

CHAPTER 3

Other Resources

Asthma affects as many as fifteen million Americans. Many of them have a mild form of the disease, and its treatment is easily managed. Many others, however, have more severe asthma requiring frequent medical attention. In some cases, the asthma is extremely difficult to control. For these people, their asthma takes them to the emergency room of their local hospital more than once a year, and sometimes they must be hospitalized for a week or more.

That may appear to be a rather bleak picture, but the fact is that most people with asthma eventually learn to bring it under control through a personal program of treatment that has been prescribed by their doctor and has been faithfully followed. Most people with asthma live normal and relatively comfortable lives.

As we saw in the last chapter, there is an ever-growing number of new medicines available to meet the needs of today's asthma patient. As we will see in Chapter 5, persons with asthma can also avail themselves of a sizable body of literature that covers subjects such as diagnosis, triggers, medications, family support, and breathing exercises.

This chapter focuses on the diverse group of healthcare professionals asthma patients may encounter, as well as the numerous organizations and associations that have evolved to help the millions of people with asthma. The chapter is divided into three sections. The first concerns the professionals, the individuals who play specific roles in your healthcare, from the familiar family doctor and nurse to specialists like the allergist, chest specialist, cardiologist, and hospital discharge planner. It is in this section that you will meet the professionals who are, in essence, the guides who will help you negotiate the sometimes complicated medical landscape.

The second section introduces the organizations out there that may be of additional help to you. Some of them, like the Asthma and Allergy Foundation of America, exist especially to aid patients with asthma (as well as concerned doctors and other healthcare professionals who treat asthma). Other organizations focus on areas of concern that overlap those of many asthma sufferers, such as the American Lung Association, whose interest is lung disease in general, including asthma. Some of these associations offer group therapy, many have newsletters or other publications, many sponsor research, and virtually all can offer you some valuable services in getting the best care possible.

The third section provides information on camping programs for children with asthma and allergies. Such programs are conducted throughout the United States. Summer camps for children with asthma vary in scope and duration and the kinds of services offered—with proper guidance, you should be able to find the one that is right for your child.

As a patient or parent trying to manage the course of a life-long illness like asthma, you are forced over time to deal with a series of events, each with its own surprises. In this chapter you will get a broader picture of the services that are out there to help you respond, and of the kinds of specific help available from medical professionals or from concerned national or local organizations.

The Professionals

We live in a world where specialization rules. While the notion of a "family doctor" or general practitioner has made a notable comeback in recent years, the prevailing wisdom still argues strongly for expert consultation, especially when your complaint is unusual or serious.

If your asthma is diagnosed as mild in nature, your family doctor, with the consultation of a specialist, is probably quite capable of providing you with the medical care you need. (These days, by the way, the family doctor, perhaps a general practitioner or internist, is often termed the "primary care physician.") However, even if the asthma is mild, we recommend that your famly doctor at least consult with a specialist. If, on the other hand, the asthma is puzzling or difficult to control, your doctor should refer you to the care of a specialist.

Today there are many medical specialties which, as organized groups, set the rules for the specialized training and examinations that are required for doctors to become "board certified" as specialists. Among the specialists that you, as an asthma patient, may work with are the chest specialist, allergist, or cardiologist. If your child has serious asthma he or she may have to see a pediatric allergist or pulmonary specialist. Each medical professional must undergo a different period of required training and different types of examinations; the requirements are, of course, tailored to the nature of the discipline and are meant to ensure that those certified are highly competent in their fields. To bring doctors up to the desired standards of excellence and knowledge, various certifying bodies or boards often require years of practice under supervision and set very difficult examinations. In fact, "board certification" in a given area of medical knowledge implies expertise in that field that is well above the level required for state licensing as a doctor.

However, in an era when specialization is more and more the rule, we do well to remember that many older physicians, despite having devoted much of their professional lives to certain fields of human illness, are not necessarily "board certified" even though they may share or perhaps even surpass the expertise of the younger, certified doctor. Thus, while it is important to be aware of your doctor's fields of certification and listings in specialty directories, such factors do not tell the whole story.

THE INTERNIST: An internist is a specialist in internal medicine. Becoming an internist involves spending a minimum of three years after being licensed as a doctor getting accredited training in the broad field of internal medicine. The three-year period is often divided into a year of internship and two of residency, but in any case the thirty-six months of training will have included at least twenty-four months of "meaningful patient responsibility." Then the internist must pass a stiff board examination.

THE CHEST SPECIALIST: Having earned the right to be called an internist, the doctor who wishes to become a chest specialist must then complete two additional years of full-time graduate training in his field. As with all specialties, there is also a written examination that must be passed, and the candidate must have clinical competence attested to by the director of the respective program he or she attends. In this case, the result is a high level of expertise in the diagnosis and management of respiratory disorders.

THE ALLERGIST: If your asthma is believed to include allergies, as so many cases are, your doctor should recommend that you consult an allergist, a doctor with special training in the diagnosis and treatment of allergic diseases. The allergist is a board-certified internist or pediatrician who has taken an additional two years of training as a specialist in allergy and immunology and is required to have knowledge of and experience in allergic and immunologic diseases, although most specialize in only one of these areas. The allergist can conduct various diagnostic procedures to assess whether (or to what degree) allergies are affecting your asthma. Some of those diagnostic procedures include skin tests, inhalation challenges, and blood tests.

The training of an allergist, like all medical doctors, is a lengthy process. In this instance it involves at least nine years of intense study. This includes medical school, followed by three years of training in internal medicine or pediatrics, which is then followed by specialized training in allergy and immunology known as a fellowship. Because the trained allergist/clinical immunologist is an internist or pediatrician in addition to having a special competency for treating asthma and allergy, he or she has the capability of a primary care physican who can effectively manage the comprehensive health care needs of patients with asthma and allergies.

A qualified allergist can be found through your county medical society or a local accredited hospital. The American Board of Allergy and Immunology will be willing to help (215-349-9466), as will the American Board of Medical Specialties in Chicago, Illinois.

THE PEDIATRICIAN: A pediatrician may be called in if the patient is an infant, although many allergists are trained in pediatrics. Pediatrics is an independent board-certified specialty. It, too, involves years of formal education, internship, and residency beyond the M.D. degree.

THE PEDIATRIC PULMONARY SPECIALIST: If the asthma is considered serious, a pediatric pulmonary specialist may be consulted. These specialists follow essentially the same five-year procedure (after completion of medical school) described above to become board certified. They're initially trained as primary care physicians and then enter the specialty of pediatrics, where they specialize in diseases that affect lung function of infants.

THE CARDIOLOGIST: A cardiologist, or heart specialist, may be called in if the heart or blood vessels have been damaged by the asthma. A subspecialist within the field of internal medicine, the cardiologist is able to use such diagnostic techniques as electrocardiography (ECG), echocardiography, exercise testing, cardiac catheterization, and angiography to assess damage to the heart and blood vessels.

If you have any difficulty in finding a qualified chest specialist or cardiologist, check with your county medical society or a local accredited hospital. The American Lung Association can help regarding a chest specialist and the American Heart Association with a cardiologist, as can other organizations discussed in the second section of this chapter.

THE NUTRITIONIST OR REGISTERED DIETICIAN: The nutritionist or registered dietician can provide the background that you may need to understand the principles and methods of achieving a properly regulated diet, can counsel you in the proper use of an elimination diet, and, if relevant, help supervise your weight-loss program.

OTHER HEALTHCARE PROFESSIONALS: There are a multitude of other healthcare providers whom you may meet in your travels across the medical landscape. If you are hospitalized and should require any special services as the time to go home approaches, you are likely to make the acquaintance of a *discharge planner.* The discharge planner is responsible for coordinating the services you will require for the transition from hospital environment to home. This responsibility runs the gamut from helping you fill out forms, to arranging for necessary equipment, to helping you cope with complex financial or family circumstances. The discharge planner may also provide you with some patient-education materials that are basically reminders to help you follow the doctor's instructions. Although the job designation is a relatively new one, social workers or nurses have long handled such responsibilities, and continue to do so.

In some cases serious problems in our lives may indirectly affect our health. When the stress of chronic problems builds over time, it may affect your health adversely by aggravating an existing problem, such as asthma. When the asthma patient is a child and the asthma is severe and not well managed, the illness not only may affect the child's self-esteem, but it may create problems within the family as well. In some families the stress of treating the asthma patient has aggravated other existing family problems, which only made the management of the asthma all the more difficult. In these instances, a *family* or *psychiatric social worker* can be called in. Many case histories have shown that the treatment of the asthma patient was positively affected by the quality of support offered by the family. As a result, it's preferred that the social worker be experienced in dealing with families that have experienced a disabling long-term illness.

In cases where depression or other mental health problems arise, a *psychologist* or *psychiatrist* may be consulted (the psychologist has a Ph.D., the psychiatrist an M.D. with a specialty in psychiatry).

No doubt a *pharmacist* will fill your prescription for drugs, and he or she is a valuable source of information regarding the medication, its effects and side effects. The pharmacist can also answer questions if there are things you don't understand.

Whether you are lucky enough to have to meet only a few of these players or have occasion to meet all of them, they, along with nurses, orderlies, and other personnel in hospitals, clinics, and doctors' offices you may visit, constitute the team assembled to help treat your asthma and related health problems. They are here to help you: ask them your questions, and develop as close and familiar a relationship with them as you find it useful to do with any expert to whom you look for guidance.

The Organizations

The organizations listed are designed to provide help, whether in the form of publications or consultation services, but they require that you make the first move. So, place that call, write that letter, or follow up on that lead. If their concerns are yours, drop a line or telephone any of the following organizations, especially if they are in your area.

While the attempt in this chapter is to cite the useful services these organizations offer you, space limitations do not allow for including everything. Once you have contacted one or more of these organizations, you may discover that they are sources, directly or indirectly, of a variety of kinds of help. They may offer you access to support groups or therapy, to lectures, and to any number of services.

Check your yellow pages, too, for local organizations. Ask your doctor or nurse. If your child has asthma, ask the nurse for the names of parents in similar situations who might be helpful.

There are many other people like you out there. It is important that you not feel isolated: get to know your peers; they will understand you. And get all the help you can in dealing with your asthma or the asthma of someone in your family.

THE AMERICAN ACADEMY OF ALLERGY AND IMMUNOLOGY
611 East Wells Street
Milwaukee, Wisconsin 53202
(414) 272-6071

This organization serves the public in a number of ways, primarily educational. The academy produces a series of pamphlets on asthma and allergies (Tips to Remember Series—see page 155), as well as the *Asthma & Allergy Advocate,* which is a one-page newsletter published quarterly for the allergy sufferer. Each issue contains features on such topics as "What's New in Allergy Research?," "New Drugs for the Treatment of Asthma and Hay Fever," and "Reports on Controversial Allergy Techniques," In addition, it publishes a brochure, "The Role of the Allergist," which defines asthma, allergies and the immune system, the scope of allergic disease, whom it affects and why, and the role of the allergist in patient management. Another publication is the "Helpful Hints for the Allergic Patient," a six-page booklet that answers the most common questions patients ask about asthma and allergic diseases. The academy also makes available "Adverse Reactions to Foods," a booklet covering problem foods and food additives, diagnosis, treatment, and a glossary of terms. Inquire as to the price of publications, but they are usually made available in bulk quantity.

AMERICAN CAMPING ASSOCIATION
Bradford Woods
Martinsville, Indiana 46151-7902
(317) 342-8456

The American Camping Association (ACA) has over 5,000 members and thirty-two local chapters or sections nationwide. For parents needing help to understand organized camping and/or to select the right kind of camp experience for their child, it publishes the *Parents' Guide to Accredited Camps,* which lists over 2,000 ACA-accredited camps. You may purchase the current guide by calling (800) 428-CAMP or consult your local library. For more personal consultation regarding the best camp for children with asthma in your area, contact your local ACA office.

AMERICAN LUNG ASSOCIATION
1740 Broadway
New York, New York 10019
(212) 315-8700

This organization was founded in 1904 to fight tuberculosis, but today it works for the prevention and control of all lung diseases, including asthma, and for the quality care of lung disease patients. There are approximately 150 local and state Lung Associations across the country. As educational organizations, Lung Associations carry out public health education, support medical and social research, and stimulate community action needed to control and prevent lung disease. Upon request, they will send a variety of educational materials dealing with asthma and other lung diseases. Among their many other services, they can direct you to a suitable summer camp in your area for the child with asthma.

ALABAMA

ALA OF ALABAMA
P.O. Box 55209
Birmingham, Alabama 35255
(205) 933-8821

ALA OF SOUTHWEST ALABAMA
(205) 433-1849

ALASKA

ALA OF ALASKA
P.O. Box 103056
Anchorage, Alaska 995100-3056
(907) 276-LUNG

ARIZONA

ARIZONA LUNG ASSOCIATION
102 W. McDowell Road
Phoenix, Arizona 85003-1213
(602) 258-7505

ARKANSAS

ALA OF ARKANSAS
P.O. Box 3857
Little Rock, Arkansas 722003
(501) 374–3726

CALIFORNIA

ALA OF CALIFORNIA
424 Pendleton Way
Oakland, California 94621–2189
(415) 638–LUNG

ALA OF ALAMEDA COUNTY
(415) 893–5474

ALA OF CENTRAL CALIFORNIA
(209) 266–LUNG

ALA OF CONTRA COSTA–SOLANO
(415) 935–0472

LONG BEACH LUNG ASSOCIATION
(213) 436–9873

ALA OF LOS ANGELES COUNTY
(213) 935–LUNG

ALA OF MONTEREY, SANTA CRUZ, &
   SAN LUIS OBISPO COUNTIES
(408) 757–LUNG

ALA OF ORANGE COUNTY
(714) 835–LUNG

PASADENA LUNG ASSOCIATION
(818) 793–4148

ALA OF REDWOOD EMPIRE
(707) 527-LUNG

ALA OF RIVERSIDE COUNTY
(714) 682-LUNG

ALA OF SACRAMENTO-EMIGRANT TRAILS
(916) 444-LUNG or
(916) 444-5900

ALA OF SAN BERNARDINO, INYO &
  MONO COUNTIES
(714) 884-LUNG

ALA OF SAN DIEGO & IMPERIAL COUNTIES
(619) 297-3901

ALA OF SAN FRANCISCO
(415) 543-4410

ALA OF SAN MATEO COUNTY
(415) 349-1111 or
(415) 349-1600

ALA OF SANTA BARBARA COUNTY
(805) 963-1426

ALA OF SANTA CLARA-SAN BENITO COUNTIES
(408) 998-LUNG

ALA OF SUPERIOR CALIFORNIA
(916) 345-LUNG

ALA OF THE VALLEY-LODE COUNTIES
(209) 478-1888

ALA OF VENTURA COUNTY
(805) 643-2189

COLORADO

ALA OF COLORADO
1600 Race Street
Denver, Colorado 80206–1198
(303) 388–4327

CONNECTICUT

ALA OF CONNECTICUT
45 Ash Street
East Hartford, Connecticut 06108
(203) 289–5401

DELAWARE

ALA OF DELAWARE
10021 Gilpin Avenue #202
Wilmington, Delaware 19806
(302) 655–7258

DISTRICT OF COLUMBIA

DISTRICT OF COLUMBIA LUNG ASSOCIATION
475 H Street N.W.
Washington, D.C. 20001
(202) 682–LUNG

FLORIDA

ALA OF FLORIDA
P.O. Box 8127
Jackson, Florida 32239–8127
(904) 743–2933

ALA OF BROWARD–GLADES–HENDRY
(305) 524–4657

ALA OF CENTRAL FLORIDA
(305) 898–3401,2

ALA OF DADE-MONROE
(305) 377-1771

GULF COAST LUNG ASSOCIATION
(813) 347-6133

ALA OF SOUTHEAST FLORIDA
(305) 659-7644

ALA OF SOUTHWEST FLORIDA
(813) 275-7577

GEORGIA

ALA OF GEORGIA
2452 Spring Road
Smyrna, Georgia 30080
(404) 434-LUNG

ALA OF ATLANTA
(404) 872-9653

HAWAII

ALA OF HAWAII
245 N. Kukui Street
Honolulu, Hawaii 96817
(808) 537-5966

IDAHO

IDAHO LUNG ASSOCIATION
2621 Camas Street
Boise, Idaho 83705
(208) 344-6567

ILLINOIS

CHICAGO LUNG ASSOCIATION
1440 W. Washington Boulevard
Chicago, Illinois 60607-1878
(312) 243-2000

ALA OF ILLINOIS
P.O. Box 2576
Springfield, Illinois 62708
(217) 528-3441

ALA OF DuPAGE & McHENRY COUNTIES
(312) 469-2400

ILLINOIS VALLEY LUNG ASSN.
(309) 688-8212

LAKE COUNTY LUNG ASSN.
(312) 623-1805

ALA OF MID-EASTERN ILLINOIS
(815) 844-3480

ALA OF NORTH CENTRAL ILLINOIS
(312) 553-7000

INDIANA

ALA OF INDIANA
8777 Purdue Road #310
Indianapolis, Indiana 46268-3109
(317) 872-9685

ALA OF CENTRAL INDIANA
(317) 872-9685

ALA OF NORTH CENTRAL INDIANA
(219) 287-2321

ALA OF NORTHEAST INDIANA
(219) 426-1170

ALA OF NORTHWEST INDIANA
(219) 769-4264

ALA OF SOUTHWEST INDIANA
(812) 422-3402

IOWA

ALA OF IOWA
1321 Walnut Street
Des Moines, Iowa 50309
(515) 243–1225

KANSAS

ALA OF KANSAS
P.O. Box 4426
Topeka, Kansas 66604–2419
(913) 272–9290

KENTUCKY

ALA OF KENTUCKY
P.O. Box 969
Louisville, Kentucky 40201–0969
(502) 363–2652

LOUISIANA

ALA OF LOUISIANA
333 St. Charles Avenue #500
New Orleans, Louisiana 70130–3180
(504) 523–LUNG

MAINE

ALA OF MAINE
128 Sewall Street
Augusta, Maine 04330
(207) 622–6394

MARYLAND

ALA OF MARYLAND
Heaver Plaza
1301 York Road #705
Lutherville, Maryland 21093-6010
(301) 494-1100

MASSACHUSETTS

ALA OF MASSACHUSETTS
803 Summer Street, 3rd Floor
South Boston, Massachusetts 02127–1609
(617) 269–9720

ALA OF BOSTON
(617) 269-9720

ALA OF CENTRAL MASSACHUSETTS
(617) 756–5749

ALA OF ESSEX COUNTY
(617) 887–6055

ALA OF MIDDLESEX COUNTY
(617) 272–2866

**NORFOLK COUNTY-NEWTON LUNG
   ASSOCIATION**
(617) 668-6729

**ALA OF SOUTHEASTERN
   MASSACHUSETTS**
(617) 947-7204

ALA OF WESTERN MASSACHUSETTS
(413) 737–3506

MICHIGAN

ALA OF SOUTHEAST MICHIGAN
18860 West Ten Mile Road
Southfield, Michigan 48075
(313) 559–5100

ALA OF MICHIGAN
(517) 484–4541

ALA OF GENESEE VALLEY
(313) 232-3177

MINNESOTA

ALA OF MINNESOTA
614 Portland Avenue
St. Paul, Minnesota 55102
(612) 227-8014

ALA OF HENNEPIN COUNTY
(612) 871-7332

ALA OF RAMSEY COUNTY
(612) 224-4901

MISSISSIPPI

MISSISSIPPI LUNG ASSN.
P.O. Box 9865
Jackson, Mississippi 39206-9865
(601) 362-5453

MISSOURI

ALA OF EASTERN MISSOURI
1118 Hampton Avenue
St. Louis, Missouri 63139-3147
(314) 645-5505

ALA OF WESTERN MISSOURI
2007 Broadway
Kansas City, Missouri 64108
(816) 842-5242

MONTANA

ALA OF MONTANA
825 Helena Avenue
Helena, Montana 59601
(406) 442-6556

NEBRASKA

ALA OF NEBRASKA
8901 Indian Hills Drive #107
Omaha, Nebraska 68114–4057
(402) 393–2222

NEVADA

ALA OF NEVADA
P.O. Box 7056
Reno, Nevada 89510–7056
(702) 323–LUNG

NEW HAMPSHIRE

ALA OF NEW HAMPSHIRE
P.O. Box 1014
Manchester, New Hampshire 03105
(603) 669–2411

NEW JERSEY

ALA OF NEW JERSEY
1600 Route 22 East
Union, New Jersey 07083
(201) 687–9340

ALA OF CENTRAL NEW JERSEY
(201) 388–4556

DELAWARE–RARITAN LUNG ASSN.
(609) 452–2112

NEW MEXICO

ALA OF NEW MEXICO
216 Truman N.E.
Albuquerque, New Mexico 87108
(505) 265–0732

NEW YORK

BROOKLYN LUNG ASSN.
165 Cadman Plaza East #210
Brooklyn, New York 11201
(718) 624-8531

NEW YORK LUNG ASSOCIATION
22 East 40th Street
New York, New York 10016
(212) 889-3370

QUEENSBORO LUNG ASSOCIATION
112-25 Queens Boulevard
Flushing, New York 11375
(718) 263-5656

ALA OF NEW YORK STATE
8 Mountain View Avenue
Albany, New York 12205-2899
(518) 459-4197

ALA OF CENTRAL NEW YORK
(315) 422-6142

ALA-FINGER LAKES REGION
(716) 442-4260

ALA-HUDSON VALLEY
(914) 949-2150

ALA OF MID-NEW YORK
(315) 735-9225

ALA OF NASSAU-SUFFOLK
(516) 231-LUNG

ALA OF WESTERN NEW YORK
(716) 886-4655

NORTH CAROLINA

ALA OF NORTH CAROLINA
P.O. Box 27985, Main Office
Raleigh, North Carolina 27611-7985
(919) 832-8326

NORTH DAKOTA

ALA OF NORTH DAKOTA
P.O. Box 5004
Bismarck, North Dakota 58502-5004
(701) 223-5613

OHIO

ALA OF OHIO
P.O. Box 16677
Columbus, Ohio 43216-1700
(614) 279-1700

ALA OF MIAMI VALLEY
(513) 222-8391

ALA OF NORTHERN OHIO
(216) 361-8000

ALA OF NORTHWESTERN OHIO
(419) 255-2378

ALA OF SOUTHWESTERN OHIO
(513) 751-3650

ALA OF STARK-WAYNE
(216) 456-8275

OKLAHOMA

ALA OF OKLAHOMA
P.O. Box 53303
Oklahoma City, Oklahoma 73152
(405) 524-8471

ALA OF GREEN COUNTRY OKLAHOMA
(918) 747-3441

OREGON

ALA OF OREGON
P.O. Box 115
Portland, Oregon 97208
(503) 224-5145

PENNSYLVANIA

ALA OF PENNSYLVANIA
P.O. Box 4213
Harrisburg, Pennsylvania 17111-0213
(717) 564-4850

ALA OF BERKS COUNTY
(215) 373-0253

ALA OF BUCKS COUNTY
(215) 343-6420

CENTRAL PENNSYLVANIA LUNG &
HEALTH SERVICE ASSN.
(717) 234-5991

CHRISTMAS SEAL LEAGUE
AMERICAN LUNG ASSN. AFFILIATE
(412) 621-0400

ALA OF DELAWARE/CHESTER
COUNTIES
(215) 692-4233

ALA OF LANCASTER COUNTY
(717) 397-5203

ALA OF LEHIGH VALLEY
(215) 867-4100

ALA OF NORTHEAST PENNSYLVANIA
(814) 346-1784

ALA OF NORTHWEST PENNSYLVANIA
(814) 454-0109

ALA OF PHILADELPHIA &
  MONTGOMERY COUNTY
(215) 735-2200

SOUTH ALLEGHENIES LUNG ASSN.
(814) 536-7245

ALA OF S. CENTRAL PENNSYLVANIA
(717) 845-3639

ALA OF SOUTHWESTERN
  PENNSYLVANIA
(412) 834-7450

PUERTO RICO

ASOCIACIÓN PUERTORRIQUENA
  DEL PULMON
GPO Box 3468
San Juan, Puerto Rico 00936
(809) 765-5664

RHODE ISLAND

RHODE ISLAND LUNG ASSN.
10 Abbott Park Place
Providence, Rhode Island 02903-3703
(401) 421-6487

SOUTH CAROLINA

ALA OF SOUTH CAROLINA
1817 Gadsden Street
Columbia, South Carolina 29201
(803) 765-9066

SOUTH DAKOTA

SOUTH DAKOTA LUNG ASSN.
208 E. 13th Street
Sioux Falls, South Dakota 57102
(605) 336-7222

TENNESSEE

ALA OF TENNESSEE
P.O. Box 399
Nashville, Tennessee 37202-0399
(615) 329-1151

TEXAS

ALA OF TEXAS
3520 Executive Center Dr. #G-100
Austin, Texas 78731-1606
(512) 343-0502

ALA-DALLAS AREA
(214) 521-2183

ALA/SAN JACINTO AREA
(713) 963-9935

UTAH

ALA OF UTAH
19300 South 1100 East
Salt Lake City, Utah 84106-2317
(801) 484-4456

VERMONT

VERMONT LUNG ASSN.
30 Farrell Street
South Burlington, Vermont 05401
(802) 863-6817

VIRGINIA

ALA OF VIRGINIA
P.O. Box 7065
Richmond, Virginia 23221–0065
(804) 355–3295

ALA OF NORTHERN VIRGINIA
(703) 591–4131

VIRGIN ISLANDS

ALA OF THE VIRGIN ISLANDS
P.O. Box 974
St. Thomas, Virgin Islands 00801
(809) 774–2077

WASHINGTON

ALA OF WASHINGTON
2625 3rd Avenue
Seattle, Washington 98121
(206) 441–5100

WEST VIRGINIA

ALA OF WEST VIRGINIA
P.O. Box 3980
Charleston, West Virginia 25339
(304) 342–6600

WISCONSIN

ALA OF WISCONSIN
10001 West Lisbon Avenue
Milwaukee, Wisconsin 53222
(414) 463–3232

WYOMING

ALA OF WYOMING
P.O. Box 1128
Cheyenne, Wyoming 82003–1128
(307) 638–6342

THE ASTHMA AND ALLERGY FOUNDATION OF AMERICA
1302 18th Street N.W.
Suite 303
Washington, D.C. 20023
(202) 265–0265

The national headquarters of the foundation provides staff support for a voluntary health organization that has chapters and support groups throughout the country. The national office provides information about asthma and allergic diseases needed by professionals, patients, and the general public. It produces and disseminates valuable publications and other educational aids to groups and organizations, publishes the *Asthma and Allergy Advance,* which is the only regular newspaper in the country devoted to the interests of asthma and allergic diseases. It also coordinates a broad range of education and fund-raising programs through local chapters.

ASTHMATIC CHILDREN'S FOUNDATION OF NEW YORK, INC.
15 Spring Valley Road
Ossining, New York 10562
(914) 762–2110

The Asthmatic Children's Foundation is a nonprofit corporation dedicated to the treatment and rehabilitation of children severely afflicted with asthma. It is primarily for asthmatic children who reside in the northeastern part of the United States. The center is staffed on a full-time basis and has a capacity of forty-one beds, five of which are part of isolation rooms. Over a third of the staff are doctors, registered nurses, and other degreed professionals. Providing care twenty-four hours a day, 365 days a year, the program interweaves medical, psychological, and social work disciplines. Each child is involved in development programs of hygiene and social interaction, which include mainstreaming into the Ossining school system under the constant supervision of the foundation staff. The foundation publishes the *Journal of Asthma* six times a year ($65/year). It also publishes several pamphlets on topics such as the asthmatic's diet, breathing exercises, medications, and parents of children with asthma. For more information or applications for admission, write to the foundation.

NATIONAL CENTER FOR HEALTH EDUCATION
30 East 29th Street
New York, New York 10016–7901
(212) 769–1886

Since 1975 the National Center for Health Education (NCHE) has served the public's need for health education by collaborating with private and government organizations in national, state, and local settings. Through its efforts to improve the healthful living potential for all Americans, the NCHE links the work of practitioners, professionals, educators, managers, communicators, and decision-makers in order to focus on school health education, workplace health promotion, and the development of a nationwide network in community health communications. As part of its educational efforts, NCHE makes available a source book—*The Selective Guide*—which contains information about print and audiovisual materials related to asthma and asthma-related issues.

THE NATIONAL FOUNDATION FOR ASTHMA, INC.
P.O. Box 30069
Tucson, Arizona 85751–0069
(602) 323–6046

The National Foundation for Asthma (NFA) was incorporated in 1949 to provide health services for asthmatics, especially for those who encountered financial hardships. Since that time, thousands of asthmatic children and adults have benefited from NFA. A doctor's written referral is necessary before receiving treatment through the NFA. Services for patients approved by the NFA—asthma education, physical therapy, breathing retraining, smoking cessation classes, biofeedback, counseling, skin testing, allergy desensitization, and X-ray and lab work—are provided at the Tucson Medical Center.

NATIONAL INSTITUTE OF ALLERGY AND INFECTIOUS DISEASES

National Institutes of Health
Building 10
Bethesda, Maryland 20892
(301) 496–4000

The National Institute of Allergy and Infectious Diseases (NAID), one of the National Institutes of Health and a tax-supported government agency, has the primary responsibility for the scientific investigation of allergies and infectious diseases, especially as they affect the respiratory system. The mission of the institute is to conduct and support research to increase knowledge about allergic responses and to develop new and improved techniques for diagnosing and treating allergic and infectious diseases affecting the respiratory system. It also tests and evaluates new knowledge and techniques that show promise of improving diagnosis and therapy. It supports the training of scientists, clinicians, and teachers in this field. Finally, it conducts a comprehensive program of education to inform the general public and health professionals about research and clinical advances related to any of the subjects under study by the various divisions of the institute.

NATIONAL JEWISH CENTER FOR IMMUNOLOGY AND RESPIRATORY MEDICINE

1400 Jackson Street
Denver, Colorado 80206
(800) 222–LUNG

The National Jewish Center for Immunology and Respiratory Medicine is recognized internationally as a leading medicine institute for studying and treating respiratory, allergic, and immune-system diseases. With 85 full-time physicians and scientists and a total staff of 1,000, the National Jewish Center brings a multidisciplinary approach to these medical problems. It accepts patients through doctor referrals and disseminates information to the public on respiratory diseases.

Registered nurses at the center's LUNG LINE Information Service provide answers to questions about lung diseases. The nurses are prepared to answer questions about early detection, care, and prevention of respiratory diseases, including asthma, chronic bronchitis, and food allergies. They can also provide answers to such questions as "Are there any new drugs for asthma?" or "What type of air filtering system should I use in my home?" The information service is available toll-free to callers at (800) 222–LUNG. Callers from within Colorado can also reach the service by calling (303) 355–LUNG.

The center publishes two quarterly newsletters: *New Directions* for the lay public and *Update* for doctors who have referred patients to the center. In addition, they publish a number of pamphlets such as "Healthy Breathing" and "Allergy." For more information about these and other pamphlets, call the LUNG LINE.

NATIONAL REHABILITATION INFORMATION CENTER
4407 Eighth Street N.E.
Washington, D.C. 20017
(800) 34–NARIC
(202) 635–5826

The National Rehabilitation Information Center (NARIC) is the largest single source of information on disability-related research, support services, and consumer products in the country. NARIC gathers, manages, and indexes information on almost every subject related to disabilities. The organization produces a listing of over 14,000 commercially available products that can make life easier for persons with respiratory disorders. Contact them if you need information on such products as atomizers, respirators, air purifiers, humidifiers, and nebulizers.

NATIONAL SELF-HELP CLEARINGHOUSE
33 West 42nd Street
New York, New York 10036
(212) 840-7606

The National Self-Help Clearinghouse is a referral center for all sorts of support groups. It will advise you on professional organizations, community organizations, and community programs related to your specific needs. The organization also publishes and distributes a directory. Write the Clearinghouse for further information.

RESOURCES FOR CHILDREN WITH SPECIAL NEEDS
200 Park Avenue South, Suite 816
New York, New York 10003
(212) 677-4650

This organization is a comprehensive information, referral, advocacy, and support center for parents and professionals in search of programs and services for newborns and children up to twenty-one years of age who have learning, developmental, emotional, or physical disabilities. One of the many services it provides is an annual guide to camps for children with special needs. This organization serves the needs primarily of New York City residents. However, there are many other organizations in other cities that may be listed in your telephone directory under a similiar heading—"Special Needs for Children."

Summer Camps for Children with Asthma

The summer camp experience for children has long been a part of American lore. Along with standard camping programs, in recent years we have seen the growth of specialized camps—most notably, those dealing with sports or music. In addition, another sort of specialty camp has surfaced—camps with programs for children with a physical impairment.

In response to a demand for more camps that could effectively and responsibly answer the needs of children with asthma, some local chapters of the American Lung Association began to establish summer camp programs in 1967. Over the years the American Lung Association has established or supported numerous camping programs that vary in scope and duration for children with mild and severe asthma problems.

The questions for the parent are: What kind of camp should I send my child to, and where is it located? The first person to consult for advice about a summer camp for your child is the doctor treating the child. Because the doctor knows what the child's medical needs are, he or she would have some specific advice as to what services the camp should provide to meet those needs. Once you have spoken to your doctor, contact the local chapter of your American Lung Association (see pages 96–112). The ALA has established guidelines, as defined by its Pediatric and Adult Lung Disease Committee, that spell out very specific criteria for the establishment of any summer camp that accepts children with asthma. If these criteria are not met, it doesn't receive the support of the ALA. Other organizations that would be helpful are your local chapter of the Asthma and Allergy Foundation of America and the American Camping Association.

It should be noted here that, except for severe cases of asthma, children should be encouraged to attend regular group activities such as camps, school physical education programs, and recreational programs. Those camps with a nurse or physician on call, as well as support services, often are appropriate for most children with mild asthma. Whenever possible, the best policy is not to segregate children with asthma into special recreational programs. Since these children need to feel that they belong with their peers, parents are urged to enroll them in normal activities as much as possible.

However, for parents who choose a summer camp that specializes in children with asthma and allergies, it is recommended that they obtain the following information:

- Is a doctor available on a full-time basis (at the camp twenty-four hours a day)? Is the doctor an allergist? Pediatrician? Chest specialist? Does the staff include any respiratory therapists?
- Is there a fully equipped infirmary? Does it have an isolation ward?
- In an emergency, is there accesss to a nearby medical center or hospital? How far away (in minutes) is the facility?
- Does the camp have appropriate medications and equipment, since transportation to a hospital may be delayed or otherwise impeded?
- Does an emergency pack, suitable for handling both asthma- and non-asthma-related emergencies, accompany groups on outings or overnights? Does a qualified member of the medical staff accompany such groups?
- Will medicine and injections be given on specific schedules provided by the parent?

CAMP OBJECTIVES: The objectives for the child's camping experience should focus on a number of items. First, it should provide a safe camping experience the child cannot get elsewhere because of his or her disease. Second, it should prepare the child to "graduate" to a regular camp. Third, it should educate the child about the management of asthma. Specifically, it should help the child identify and react appropriately to early warning signals of an acute asthma episode, identify and avoid known asthma triggers, properly use relaxation techniques, choose alternative behavior patterns designed to prevent or stop an asthma episode, improve his or her understanding of drug therapy and the appropriate use of inhalers, and enhance his or her self-esteem.

On the other hand, parents should expect from the camp staff or management a detailed assessment of their child's camp experience. In short, they should receive or ask for a report from the camp that includes a description of their child's health status, social interaction, and the asthma classes that were attended (if any were made available). If the camp experience has been successful and if the child was able to participate in all or most of the camp activities, he or she should be better prepared to attend a mainstream or "regular" camp the following summer.

CHAPTER 4

Self-Help

As we saw in Chapter 2, a program of appropriate medication is essential to bring most cases of asthma under control. However, medication alone will not solve the problem. Effective management of asthma demands the full cooperation of the patient. For example, if the patient fails to avoid those triggers that are known to be responsible for earlier asthma episodes or delays taking medication until the asthma attack is well under way, he or she may find not only that the medication will be less effective but that asthma episodes will be more severe. Therefore, the patient has to take responsibility for the disease; that is, he or she must cooperate with the doctor and learn as much as possible about the nature of the disease. That includes learning something about the various products and services available to the asthma patient.

In this chapter we learn about several products that are designed to help patients take their medication, such as nebulizers, inhalers, and spinhalers. Some of these products are specifically designed for children who have trouble taking almost any kind of medication. In addition to these products, we discuss the merits of keeping a diary, when and why family counseling is sometimes necessary and specific breathing exercises that help reduce the likelihood of an attack or its severity once it begins.

It should be noted that any or all of these therapies and products should not be adopted or used except with the recommendation of your doctor.

Keeping a Record

Good reporters write down everything—dates, times, places, activities. Traditionally the news story is written to answer the questions who, what, when, where, and why. In order to report to a doctor your asthma story or your child's, it's important that you, too, have the answers to these kinds of questions. A written record may be very helpful to consult.

WHAT TO WRITE: Always start with the date. Then ask yourself: When did the symptoms start? What were you or your child doing and where did the episode happen? Who or what else was there? Did the symptoms usually occur within a specific period of time after exposure to a suspected trigger? What do you think brought on the symptoms? If you feel that you genuinely don't know, guess. As you write about more and more incidents, you'll find out how right or wrong your guesses were. The most important thing is to write them down.

WHAT TO LOOK FOR: You're looking for patterns. Do certain combinations of events begin to repeat themselves? Do specific symptoms occur regularly in the same places, in the same situations, during the same kinds of weather or activities? It might be useful to record the dates of the asthmatic episodes on a calendar. If you see a constant pattern emerge of "when" they happen—for example, within an hour after coming home from school—it may lead you to the "why" in the asthma story.

At the same time, these patterns are not perfect. Because there are many triggers or culprits in the usual asthma story, these patterns will not repeat themselves precisely the same way each time. You'll keep seeing differences, but don't be discouraged. Even though the asthma attacks may at first appear to occur at random, you know they don't. Eventually you'll discover those patterns or combinations of events and activities that will be critical to a successful treatment of the asthma.

WHEN TO USE IT: Bring the journal to the doctor's office. He or she needs to know what you've learned about the circumstances that led up to the asthma attacks. In turn, you need to remember the special instructions the doctor may give you. By all means write down the kind of medication the doctor prescribes, including any of their possible side effects, and any special precautions you're to take during an attack. Don't rely on your memory. A good record ensures that you'll:

- take the correct dosages at the correct time and in the proper order.
- feel less uncertain and anxious about what to do during an asthma attack.
- remember which medications you should avoid that could provoke an attack.
- know precisely when you should notify your doctor.

WHERE TO TAKE IT: If you must go to the emergency room, take the record book with you. In these circumstances anxiety runs very high, and it is very difficult to remember clearly what the doctor needs to know and what you need to remember. Medical professionals need exact information, such as your currect medications, to treat your asthma properly. You need to know what medications you or your child has been given. It is also wise to write down the names of the doctors and nurses who treat you or your child.

A good record is also helpful when sharing information with others. Parents of asthmatic children should compare notes with other people who have children with asthma.

Family Concerns

An illness is an event in the life of the family. Depending on the character of the illness, the family may have to mobilize some or all of its physical and psychological resources to deal effectively with the demands of the trying situation. If it's a recurring disease, like asthma, it can affect the entire family over an extended period of time. Not only is the patient exposed to the impact of the disease, but different members of the family experience its impact, especially through the changes the family makes to accommodate the patient and the disease.

For children with mild asthma, the impact on the family may be minimal. However, when the child suffers from severe asthma or asthma that cannot be effectively controlled, the family—principally the parents—may be faced with a variety of problems.

SOCIAL LIFE: If the child is often sick, parents may find that they aren't free to go out evenings or weekends. If they do decide to go out, they may be unable to get a suitable babysitter. Some parents have discovered that their neighbors, babysitters, and relatives have little knowledge of asthma. Parents have learned that others are often reluctant to take the responsibility for the care of a "sick" child, even for an evening.

In these situations, it's necessary that the neighbors, babysitters, or family members be made to understand that asthma need not interfere with normal activity. They can be given a pamphlet that will explain briefly the nature of the illness and what to expect (see Chapter 5). Explicit instructions should be given so that there is no mystery as to what must be done if the child experiences any asthma symptoms. The instructions should include:

- The medication, its proper name, and the prescribed dosage.
- The time(s) it is scheduled to be taken.
- The symptoms that would warrant a call to you or the doctor—for example, if the child makes a noise breathing out, sucks in the skin about the collarbone (sign of a struggle to breathe), or takes longer to breathe out than in.

A good source of competent babysitters are families who face, or have faced, the same problem. They could be found through your doctor's practice or through a support group composed of other parents whose children have asthma. For help in finding these groups contact your local American Lung Association (see page 96).

DISCIPLINE: Parents are sometimes reluctant to punish the child who has asthma for fear that the punishment will cause an attack. While some children may wheeze because they are upset when punished, this response seldom leads to a full-blown asthma attack. On the contrary, greater harm is done when the child escapes the punishment that he or she deserves. Even though it may have been the child's strategy to avoid punishment, if the parents' policy is not to punish the child with asthma out of fear for his or her health, they send a message to the child: "We don't see you as normal." This attitude could feed into the child's dread of the asthma and, perhaps, cause him or her not to cooperate with the treatment program. Also, other children in the family may begin to resent the child who goes unpunished, which might add to that child's isolation within the family.

SELF-CARE: One of the most important aspects in the care of asthma should be the child's confidence that he or she can handle the asthma. Therefore, it's best not to refer to the child with asthma as an "asthmatic." This term portrays the child as a problem, which distorts his or her own self-picture and the attitude of others around him or her. To be known as an "asthmatic" may cause him or her to feel that the asthma is more important than he or she is. On the other hand, "a child with asthma" suggests that the child is generally healthy but has a problem which requires care.

To develop confidence that the asthma can be controlled, the child should be encouraged to understand the illness and how medication and other treatments help to control the symptoms. Instead of ignoring the early signs of asthma symptoms or feeling helpless when the asthma symptoms occur, the child should know there are several things that can be done to control the asthma:

1. The child should never fall into a pattern of pretending his symptoms will go away. The early signs of asthma symptoms should be respected, not ignored.
2. As much as possible, the child should be taught to follow his medication program closely. Depending on the age of the child, he should be given as much responsibility as possible in his own care.
3. If the child's back-up medication does not work, he should report his symptoms to his parents or his doctor before they get worse. If he repeatedly ignores his asthma symptoms, it may be helpful to have a psychiatrist or a psychiatric social worker work with him.

FAMILY STRESS: Asthma can be an expensive problem. In addition to the expense of doctor's visits, medication, and hospitalization, there are such costs as psychological counseling, special summer camps, and lost time at work. In some instances, when asthma has been difficult to manage and has involved frequent emergencies and hospitalizations, treatment can consume as much as 20 percent of a family's income. Mounting costs can cause resentment among other members of the family, and the child may experience some guilt because of the expense and inconvenience the child feels he or she has caused the family.

Asthma can also cause disruptions in the family routine that may sometimes magnify other family problems. In some families the illness of the child and existing family problems have aggravated each other to the point that they eventually are seen as one and the same. When the source of the problem lies within the family itself, and not just in the child's illness, family counseling usually becomes necessary. These situations can be painful and complicated, requiring a qualified professional, perferably someone who has had experience handling children with asthma.

Products
for
Home Use

No two cases of asthma are exactly alike. Every person with asthma will experience the illness and the treatments for it differently. The varied combination of causes or triggers, the individual program of medication, the self-help techniques which may or may not be effective, and the patient's own emotional response to the illness makes each case distinctive. For example, some people will grow tense or fearful during an attack, which will adversely affect the severity of their asthma symptoms. Other people are able to relax during an attack, which usually contributes to the relief of their symptoms.

Thus, all of these factors contribute to the varied picture of the asthma experience. Yet most asthma patients (or parents of children with asthma) share a common concern: Will they (or their child) be able to lead a normal life?

As we saw in Chapter 2, you and your doctor will create from a variety of treatment choices an appropriate plan of care that is suitable to your needs. In this chapter you'll find several different types of products and self-help strategies that are designed to help in that effort. In addition, there is information on some products that help children who have difficulty administering their medication. However, before you make any purchases or changes in your program of care, consult with your doctor.

HOW TO FIND THE PRODUCTS: Most of the products discussed in the following pages are generally available at hospital supply houses. A few can be purchased at your local drugstore. In the event that you have difficulty finding a particular item locally, write to the source cited and request a catalog, price list, and, in the case of the manufacturer, the location of a store or distributor in your area where the item can be purchased. Keep in mind that the total cost for products from a mail-order firm may be slightly higher because of handling and postage charges.

Nebulizer

A nebulizer is a machine that produces a fine spray or mist. The compressor of the nebulizer creates a mist by rapidly passing air through a liquid or by vibrating a liquid at a high frequency so the particles produced are extremely small. Much like an atomizer, aerosol, or vaporizer, a nebulizer creates a vapor from a liquid.

ADVANTAGES: Nebulizers are used in the treatment of asthma because by creating a fine mist from the liquid medication, the asthma patient can inhale the medication, which is delivered directly to the site of the problem (the airways). Inhaling medications causes the drug to act faster than oral medications, which must be swallowed. Another advantage is that, since less medication is needed when it is inhaled, fewer side effects occur. For example, patients with heart, thyroid, or high blood pressure problems prefer to inhale adrenaline-based medications (see "Bronchodilators [Inhaled]," page 48) because a potential side effect of the oral form of that medication is an accelerated heart rate.

Children and adults who are needle-shy appreciate the fact that their medication can be administered in this manner, too. The powered nebulizer is also recommended for the very young child with asthma who is unable to use a simple inhaler (see below). With the inhaler, patients must time their inhalation with the delivery of the puff from the inhalator. This coordination is difficult for many children. For the child under three years old who has been hospitalized for asthma, a nebulizer is usually always recommended as part of home treatment.

PURCHASE: The cost for a powered nebulizer is approximately $125.00, but prices vary greatly for the same machine. They are available from Devilbiss Company, Somerset, Pennsylvania 15501 (Pulmo-Aide); Mead Johnson Company, Evansville, Indiana 47721 (Maxi-Myst); and Mountain Medical Equipment, Littleton, Colorado (Medi-Mist).

MEASURING MEDICATION FOR A NEBULIZER: An inhalation treatment is prepared by placing saline (salt) solution and the bronchodilating medication in the canister of the nebulizer. It is important that before preparing the medication for the nebulizer you wash your hands thoroughly. You are going to breathe the medication directly into your lungs, so it's important that everything is clean. When measuring your medication, follow this procedure:

1. Use a clean measuring device for measuring your medication. You can use an eyedropper, teaspoon, or syringe as a measuring device.
2. Always use caution when measuring your medication. Use the exact amount of each solution as specified by your doctor.

3. If you think that you have made a mistake in measuring, empty the nebulizer and begin again.
4. If an eyedropper is supplied with your medication, it will be marked in ml (milliliters) or cc (cubic centimeters). Fill the dropper to the line that indicates the amount of medication your doctor ordered. Squeeze this amount into your nebulizer cup.
5. If your medicine is not premixed, measure the saline solution or water in the same manner as you measured your medicine.
6. Keep all medication in the refrigerator. Discard any solutions that may have changed color or formed crystals.

OPERATING A NEBULIZER: Select a comfortable area in your home where the unit can be placed and the treatments taken without interruption. Plug the cord from the compressor into a grounded electrical outlet. Do not use an extension cord if possible. Again, wash your hands thoroughly and follow these steps:

1. Prepare the medication for the nebulizer (see page 125).
2. Remove the T-piece from the nebulizer with the prescribed amount of medication.
3. Reconnect the nebulizer to the T-piece and mouthpiece/mask.
4. Connect the nebulizer to the tubing.
5. Be sure the tubing is attached to the compressor.
6. Position yourself comfortably in a sitting position.
7. Turn the compressor switch to the ON position.
8. Check to see that the medication is misting.
9. Place your lips securely around the mouthpiece or position the mask on your face; inhale slowly and as deeply as possible.
   [NOTE: If much of the medicine hits your cheeks or palate, you may not be getting the full dose. Readjust the mouthpiece until the mist is striking the back of your throat.]
10. Hold your breath for one or two seconds and then exhale slowly.
   [NOTE: If your pulse increases markedly, if you become dizzy, or if you become shaky, stop your treatment and rest for five to ten minutes. Then continue the treatment, but breathe at a slower rate. If these symptoms continue, notify your doctor.]
11. Continue to breathe slowly through the nebulizer until you have either used all the medication or have taken the treatment for the prescribed time.
12. Turn the ON/OFF switch to the OFF position.

13. If needed, cough several times to loosen and bring up any mucus or secretions. Spit the secretions into a tissue.
14. Clean your equipment according to the procedure outlined below.

CLEANING A NEBULIZER: A nebulizer that has not been kept clean may not work properly. If it does not work properly, it may not deliver the right amount of medication. Consequently, you may come to believe that your medication is not as effective as it used to be and that you need more, when in fact it is the nebulizer that is not delivering as much medication as it should. A dirty nebulizer also poses the risk of spreading bacteria that might grow on the mouthpiece. As a precaution against any infection or dysfunctioning of the nebulizer, the following cleaning steps should be observed:

AFTER EACH TREATMENT:

1. Wash your hands.
2. Rinse the mouthpiece and nebulizer under a strong stream of warm water.
3. Shake off any excess water.
4. Reassemble for the next treatment.

EACH DAY:

1. Wash your hands.
2. Disassemble the nebulizer, T-piece, and mouthpiece.
3. Wash disassembled parts in liquid detergent and warm water.
4. Rinse all the parts.
5. Shake off any excess water.
6. Air dry parts between folds of paper towels or on a clean hand towel.
7. Reassemble for use.

EVERY THIRD DAY:

1. Wash your hands.
2. Wash disassembled parts in a liquid detergent and warm water.
3. Rinse thoroughly.
4. Soak for ten minutes in Control III Disinfectant Germicide (½ ounce to 2 quarts water).
   [NOTE: The solution may be kept fourteen days in a covered container. Mark the date to discard the solution on the cover.]

5. Remove parts from the Control III. Rinse and shake off the excess water.
6. Air dry between folds of paper towels or on a clean hand towel.
7. When thoroughly dry, store in a plastic bag until ready for use.

OTHER MAINTENANCE TIPS: To keep the compressor dust free, cover it with a clean towel when not in use and do not store it on the floor. At least once a month, unscrew the filter cap and check the color of the filter. If it's dirty, replace it.

Much of this information on the use and care of the nebulizer comes from the publication "Hand-Held Nebulizers," available from the Visiting Nurse Service.

Inhaler

The instructions for the use of an inhaler differ slightly from those for a nebulizer. To begin with, the inhaler is not powered. Therefore, after putting the mouthpiece on the canister, the inhaler must be shaken for about two seconds. Then position the inhaler with the canister above the mouthpiece. It should look to be upside down. For the most effective use of an inhaler, follow these steps:

1. Stand up and hold the mouthpiece about an inch from your lips and open your mouth wide.
2. Breathe naturally with your mouth wide open. Then point the inhaler toward the back of your throat, squeeze the canister, and draw the medicine into your mouth in a steady stream. Take two seconds to inhale as deeply as you can.
3. Hold your breath for as long as you can—up to ten seconds.
4. Don't close your mouth during this procedure. If the medicine runs out of your mouth, it didn't get deep enough.
5. Wait two minutes and try it again. If the first inhalation (whiff) was successful, it will have opened the airways. The second whiff, therefore, should deliver the medicine even more effectively.

Many people report relief within five to ten minutes following this procedure. The benefits should last for at least four hours. If you use the inhaler more than five times a day—with two whiffs on each use—the asthma may be slipping out of control. In this situation, see your doctor.

MISTAKES USING THE INHALER: It seems that people make many mistakes when first using an inhaler, so be sure to follow the instructions on the package. If you are still unsure, ask your doctor or nurse. The following is a good checklist for uncovering some common mistakes:

1. Are you leaving more of the medicine in your mouth and not in your windpipes? If so, you may be inhaling too fast.
2. Are you exhaling too fast? If so, the medicine may not have had a chance to settle where it is most needed.
3. Are you forgetting to take a second whiff? If so, you may not be getting enough medicine into the expanded windpipes. Children often forget to do it twice.
4. Are you waiting at least two minutes between whiffs? If not, your medication may not be reaching where it is most needed.
5. Are you inhaling deeply at the very same time you're squeezing the inhaler? If not, you may not be taking the deep inspiration you need at the right time. Just when you are about to squeeze the inhaler, try breathing more slowly. It may be helpful to practice your timing with an inhaler that does not have any medicine in it.

Bubble Reservoir

As we said earlier, many young children have difficulty timing their inhalation with their squeezing of the inhaler. If the two discrete actions are not matched, little of the medication will reach the bronchial tubes. For the hysterical child experiencing an asthma attack this may be an impossible task.

An inexpensive device called the "bubble reservoir" was designed for children with this problem. It holds the medication spray in a plastic bubble or reservoir until the child is ready to breathe in. The child can breathe as often as necessary to inhale the spray. He or she doesn't need exact timing to get the medication into the windpipe; therefore the device eliminates the need for exact coordination required by the inhaler. Because the medication is dispersed into a chamber full of air, the unpleasant taste of the medication is diluted. The bubble reservoir also provides a float or "incentive marker" in the bubble that indicates how deeply the child is inhaling the medication. At first the float may rise very little, but as the airways open in response to the medication and the child inhales more deeply, the float will rise higher. As with the inhaler, this device is effective with children (or adults) with mild or moderate asthma.

PURCHASE: The cost of a bubble reservoir is approximately $20.00 and is available from Key Pharmaceuticals, 4400 Biscayne Blvd., Miami, Florida 33137 (Inhal-Aid). This product requires a prescription for purchase. You might also ask your doctor about a product called InspirEase, which is also available through Key Pharmaceuticals.

Tube

Older children who continue to have trouble over the years timing the release of medications from an inhaler with their inhalation may find a tube reservoir helpful. The tube is about 8 inches long and 2 inches in diameter, and it contains a puff of the aerosol medication. The puff is held in the tube until the child inhales. The patient inhales for two to three seconds, then holds his breath for ten seconds. The tube has a valve that prevents accidental release of the medication.

PURCHASE: The cost is approximately $15.00. It is available from Monaghan Medication Corporation, Plattsburgh, New York 12901 (Aero-Chamber).

Peak Flow Meter

EARLY DETECTION: One of the most important elements of any asthma treatment program is early detection of signs that an attack is imminent. Unfortunately, early changes in the reduced efficiency of the lungs are not easily detected. Frequently, when the inexperienced patient suspects something may be wrong, he or she attributes it to something else. Someone involved in heavy exercise, for example, may attribute any slight difficulty in breathing to the strain of the exercise. Another instance where early detection is a problem occurs among young children. Because of their age they are unable to reliably report or confirm respiratory changes with any accuracy.

The problem of early detection occurs even during a physical examination. While a stethoscope is designed to discover problems in the bronchial airways, it can detect a change only after the flow of air being expelled from the lungs has dropped by more than 25 percent. At this point the patient may be well into an attack, even though he or she has not yet felt a tightness in the chest or begun wheezing. Ideally, the time to treat a potential asthma attack is before the symptoms are readily apparent.

MINI-WRIGHT PEAK FLOW METER: One effective device that discovers early changes in lung function is a peak flow meter, sometimes called a huffer. The mini-Wright Peak Flow Meter measures the maximum flow rate of air from a single forced expiration, otherwise known as the peak expiratory flow (PEF). The ideal rate is related to height and age and varies greatly between individuals. You can check a chart for average values, but the best way to find your normal PEF is to check your huff (a short, hard exhalation) several times when you are feeling fine. This is your best or normal value. Then after a normal PEF is determined, you can self-test daily as instructed by your doctor and record the highest reading from each test on a daily trend chart.

If there is a change in your normal value, it means that air is not flowing from your lungs as freely as usual. If you feel fine but your PEF reading in the morning is 370 instead of the usual 420, it means something is happening. It could suggest an allergic response, the onset of a cold, or the beginning of an asthma attack. Depending on your past experience, if the reading drops to a predetermined danger zone, you can elect to take your prescribed medication to ward off the impending attack. As a matter of policy, you should always speak to your doctor about the significance of the information you gather from the huffer and how to interpret your readings properly. For example, if this pattern of early morning fall in your huff readings continued, your doctor might recommend an increase in your medication.

ADVANTAGES: Not everyone needs a huffer at home. Many people can successfully anticipate the triggers and early warning signs of their asthma attacks without one. However, lots of people with asthma use a huffer, either a mini-Wright Peak Flow Meter or a Pulmonary Monitor (see below), at home for some of the following reasons:

Early Warning: Perhaps its most important value is that it can predict an asthma attack for some people. Studies show that in some patients the peak flow will drop as early as twenty-four hours before symptoms of an attack become evident. For the patient whose asthma attacks come on quickly, this early warning allows them to start medication as soon as possible.

Detects Triggers: Besides suggesting the presence of other potential irritants in the house or work site, it can prove conclusively that cigarette smoke affects lung function. If you have any concerns about exercise, the meter can help determine what level of exercise is safe. The meter will also help confirm whether certain early clues in your body are in fact potential triggers for an asthma attack. For example, you might discover that your PEF changes shortly after you experience the same irritation with a new perfume someone is wearing in the family.

Controls Medication: It can determine whether the current level of medication is effective or needs to be changed. Furthermore, patients can see if their lung function remains stable while reducing their medication. If the peak flow rate doesn't change, they can further reduce medication levels with less risk of a relapse.

HOW TO USE: These instructions apply to both the mini-Wright Peak Flow Meter and the pulmonary monitor (see below).

1. Move the pointer to zero and hold with vent free.
2. Put the mouthpiece on your tongue and place lips around mouthpiece.
3. In a standing position blow out as hard and as fast as possible—a short, sharp blast. The meter measures your fastest huff, not your longest.
4. Wait approximately fifteen seconds and blow again. Repeat this procedure one more time.
5. Record the best effort. Do this once in the morning and once at night.

PURCHASE: Small and very portable for home use, the mini-Wright Peak Flow Meter is only 6 inches by 7½ inches by 2⅔ inches and weighs 11 ounces. It is simple to use and easily cleaned and maintained. The cost is $59.50, and it is available from Armstrong Medical Industries Inc., 3660 Commercial Avenue, P.O. Box 7, Northbrook, Illinois 60065 (800) 323–4220. Now on the market are less expensive peak flow meters suitable for home use, but they may not be as accurate as the mini-Wright. The less expensive peak flow meters can be purchased from HealthScan Products Inc., Upper Montclair, New Jersey 07043.

A Vitalograph Pulmonary Monitor is not as accurate, but it's adequate for home use, particularly by children with a peak flow over 150 liters per minute. Its cost is approximately $25.00, and it is available from Vitalograph Medical Instrumentation, 8347 Quivira Road, Lenexa, Kansas 66215 (800) 255-6626. For example, there are two kinds of peak flow monitors—a standard monitor, which measures a flow range from 150 to 700 liters per minute, and a low-range monitor, which measures a flow range from 50 to 280 liters per minute. Therefore, before purchasing a peak flow meter, consult your doctor.

Spinhaler

This device is used to administer medication that comes in the form of a dry powder. Cromolyn, for example, is a dry powder in capsule form that is inhaled into the lungs using a spinhaler. (As you learned in Chapter 2, cromolyn is also available in a solution and is used in a nebulizer.)

OPERATING A SPINHALER: Place the yellow side of the capsule down in the spinhaler. Move the sleeve of the spinhaler down toward the mouthpiece and then up so that the capsule is broken. The inhalation instructions for the spinhaler are the same as for the inhaler (see page 128) with the exception that you place your mouthpiece in your mouth, not an inch away as with the inhaler. The steps are as follows:

1. Breathe out and slowly empty your lungs of air.
2. Place the spinhaler in your mouth.
3. Tilt your head back and take in as big a breathe as possible. This draws the powder into your throat and lungs.
   [NOTE: The spinhaler is so named because it rotates as you draw the airborne powder from it.]
4. Hold your breath for a few seconds after inhaling the powder.
5. Remove the mouthpiece and exhale.
6. Repeat the procedure to make sure all of the powder has been drawn from the spinhaler.

Many young children find the spinhaler easier to master than the aerosol inhaler technique. In this regard, a whistle can be attached to the spinhaler. The child should be told that the deeper he inhales, the louder the whistle will blow. He should also be told that the whistle blows only if he inhales from the spinhaler. It won't work if he blows into it.

Exercises

EARLY WARNING: For the vast number of people with asthma, asthma attacks usually do not happen suddenly, even though they may seem to on occasion. Asthma attacks are usually preceded by warning signs that give them time to take action. These signs may vary from person to person, but they generally are a light wheezing or tightness in the chest, coughing, or some restlessness while trying to sleep at night. Whatever they may be for you, it's important that you come to know what the warning signs are and when they are most likely to occur. If you have some doubt about your ability to anticipate your asthma episodes or feel unsure about a specific symptom that may be an early sign of one, it's recommended that you become familiar with the use of a peak flow meter (see page 130). These devices can measure your airflow and tell you if some abnormality is developing in your lungs.

WHAT TO DO FIRST: If your peak flow meter reading is low or, for other reasons, you suspect an asthma attack is beginning, take the medicine your doctor has prescribed to prevent the episode from getting worse. Prompt action can reduce the severity of the symptoms and reduce the possibility that you will need stronger medicines later on. In addition, when you think an episode is about to begin, breathe properly and try to relax—as difficult as it may seem—because anxiety can increase the severity of the episode. Learning how to breathe properly and relax is the subject of this section.

IMPROPER BREATHING: It's safe to say that many people do not breathe properly, especially when they are under stress. During an asthma attack, a time when the body's need for oxygen is increasing, proper breathing becomes critical. Unfortunately, many asthmatics, especially those inexperienced with their disease, don't know how to relax and breathe deeply to increase their vital capacity.

During an attack the asthma patient has to work harder to breathe. Unfortunately, many fall back on old inefficient breathing habits that rely on chest and neck muscles to do the job. As was mentioned earlier, one of the dramatic signs of an impending asthma episode for a child is when the skin is drawn in around the collarbone. This is an indication that the child is trying to increase lung capacity with the muscles in the neck and chest. This method of labored breathing often doesn't supply the body with enough oxygen, and it soon exhausts the patient. Over the years, some asthma patients who have not learned proper breathing methods develop a stooped look or rounded shoulders by breathing in this fashion. Some children even develop permanent chest deformities.

PROPER BREATHING: The proper muscles needed to do the job are the diaphragm, the muscle that separates the chest and abdomen, and the muscles between the ribs. If these muscles are used correctly, the amount of air the lungs take in and out is significantly increased—and the individual is less likely to get exhausted in the process. In fact, diaphragmatic breathing (in which you properly use the diaphragm) can strengthen the upper torso, improve posture, and make normal breathing easier and more effective. The person with asthma who learns to relax with proper breathing techniques may actually reduce the number of asthma attacks and reduce panic and fear of suffocation.

Effective deep breathing should accomplish the following:

- Improve the exchange of oxygen and carbon dioxide.
- Loosen secretions of mucus from the bronchial walls.
- Strengthen and stretch the muscles of respiration.
- Improve posture.
- Promote relaxation of the body.

Diaphragmatic Breathing

Breathing exercises should be done daily and often. For beginners, breathing exercises should be done at least three times a day for a minimum of a month. Once you have established a competence and confidence in the exercises, you can do them less often. A good practice is to do a breathing exercise first thing in the morning and just before going to bed at night. Of course, at the first sign of wheezing or while waiting for your medication to take effect, deep breathing can be helpful.

The following is one diaphragmatic breathing exercise:

1. Sit in a straight-back chair or, if your doctor agrees, lie on your back on a flat, firm surface and place a pillow under your knees.
2. Place one hand below your ribs and the other on your chest.
3. Inhale slowly through your nose for a count of two. As you inhale, your hand below your ribs should move out and your hand on your chest should remain as still as possible.
4. Exhale slowly through pursed lips for a count of four. Your hand below your ribs should move in.
   [NOTE: During the exercise, keep your upper chest as quiet as possible and your neckmuscles relaxed.]
5. Do this exercise for three to five minutes at a time.

Pursed-Lip Breathing Exercise

During an attack, your bronchial airways will grow more narrow, making it difficult to exhale and trapping some of the air in your lungs. A breathing technique called pursed-lip breathing builds up back pressure that eases more of the trapped air out (carbon dioxide) and permits more of the fresh air (oxygen) to be inhaled. It's also a good exercise whenever you are about to start a physical activity that may leave you breathless:

1. Inhale slowly through your nose.
2. Purse your lips by pretending that you have a drinking straw between your lips.
3. Breathe out slowly and evenly through the pursed lips.
4. Try to take twice as long to breathe out as you did to breathe in. [NOTE: If at any time you feel dizzy during the exercise, stop and rest for a few breaths. Once you've gained control of your breathing, stay relaxed and breathe slowly.]
5. Practice pursed-lip breathing several times a day.

Relaxation Exercise

It's recommended that you always try deep breathing to reduce tension or tightness in your chest. However, another way to relax is the following:

1. Lie on your back with your head and knees supported by pillows. Rest your arms comfortably at your sides. If this is not convenient, sit up in a chair and let your hands hang loosely at your sides.
2. Clench your fists, tighten your arms, and shrug your shoulders. Hold this for a count of two.
3. Relax for a count of four.
4. Tighten your arms and legs together and hold for a count of two.
5. Relax for a count of four.
6. Repeat this exercise several times.

Cough Control

A spell of uncontrolled coughing brought on by an asthma attack can add to your shortness of breath, tire you out, and maybe cause you some embarrassment. On the other hand, an "effective" cough can bring up some of the trapped mucus plugs and clear your airways, which will make your breathing easier. When you feel a cough coming on or you want to raise some mucus that you feel is trapped in your lungs, follow these steps:

1. Sit with your head slightly forward, feet on the floor. Breathe in deeply.
2. Hold your breath for a few seconds.
3. Cough forcefully twice in a row. The first cough loosens the mucus secretions and the second helps to bring it up.
4. Use strong tissues or a paper towel to get rid of the mucus. Swallowing mucus can upset your stomach.
5. Breathe in by sniffing gently.
   [NOTE: It's recommended that you drink plenty of fluids, as much as eight glasses per day, to thin the mucus in your lungs. Another technique to help keep the secretion thin is the use of a cool mist humidifier or vaporizer. These units add moisture to the air you breathe.]

There are several recommended publications in Chapter 5 that offer many more breathing and relaxation techniques. An excellent booklet for children or parents of children with asthma is entitled "Breathing Easy" and is available from the Asthmatic Children's Foundation (see page 112).

CHAPTER 5

Selected Print
and
Audiovisual Materials

If what you read in the previous chapters of this book made you want to know more, there is an extensive library of print and audiovisual materials available to you.

The intent of this closing chapter is to provide you with specific sources for further information beyond what you can learn from the organizations listed in Chapter 3. The first section presents the available publications, ranging from pamphlets that require only minutes to read to complex, full-length reference works. The concluding section lists audiovisual materials, including films, videocassettes, and audiocassettes on asthma.

The print section is arranged alphabetically by title. The leaflets, pamphlets, or booklets that deal with complications and risk factors associated with asthma are generally free or available at low cost. The full-length books that deal more comprehensively and in greater depth with various aspects of asthma are available in your local bookstore or library.

The audiovisual section includes materials, also arranged alphabetically by title, on a number of asthma-related concerns. Generally, these materials can be rented or purchased.

If you want to know more about your asthma, the odds are that you will find a suitable source of information listed in the following pages.

Print
Materials

This section does not attempt to provide a complete list of every available publication but rather discusses a representative selection of the best and most valuable ones available. You may find some very fine publications in your library or bookstore that are not listed here. Some are not included in these pages simply because they are not generally available. Some, perhaps, were published since this book was completed. Other materials, however, may have been reviewed and judged less useful than those that are cited in these pages. There are also a significant number of books for sale that contain information that is out of date or medically ineffective.

How to Obtain These Publications

The American Lung Association publications are available from the national office or your local chapter. (See Chapter 3 for the address of the ALA chapter in your state or city.) Books published by general trade publishers can be found in libraries or may be ordered from your local bookstore. Where the publication is available only directly from the organization that publishes it, the address, telephone number, and pertinent order information is included in the entry.

Allergies (Medicine for the Layman Series)
Kaliner, Michael, M.D.
Head, Allergic Diseases Section
Laboratory of Clinical Investigation
25 pages
U.S. Department of Health and Human Services
Public Health Service
120/80 National Institutes of Health
Bethesda, Maryland 20205

This booklet discusses the mechanisms that produce the response that we refer to as an "allergic reaction." It moves on to discuss the mediators of allergy (the chemicals released in the body), the incidence of allergy, and its treatment. It analyzes the problems of asthma and closes with a question-and-answer section that deals with a number of the most often asked questions about allergies and asthma.

The Allergy Encyclopedia
The Asthma & Allergy Foundation of America
  and Craig T. Norback
New York, New York: New American Library, 1981
258 pages
Order from: publisher or your local bookstore
ISBN: 0-452-25629-1 Paper $8.95

As one would expect from an encyclopedia, this book attempts to provide the allergy sufferer, including the asthma patient with allergies, with an overall view of this common, complex group of diseases. With the exception of the chapter on food allergies and allergy cooking, the remaining eight chapters are written by a medical doctor. The book begins by addressing itself to those most frequently asked questions about allergies and then goes into a discussion of allergies, allergens, and related terms. Chapters 3 and 4 discuss how to cope with emergencies and allergic disease and its treatment. After a discussion of the basic science of allergy, allergy research, and regional factors, the book looks at the problem of food and how to prepare food for the person with allergies. The last chapter is devoted solely to the condition of asthma. Some sections of the book are a little demanding, but the book is still accessible to a lay audience.

Allergy Products Directory (Second Edition)
Menlo Park, California: American Allergy Association, 1987
122 pages
Order from: Allergy Publications Group
P.O. Box 640
Menlo Park, California 94026
Paper $9.95

This may be the most comprehensive listing of allergy products available. It is suitable to serve as the standard, comprehensive reference source for individual allergy and asthma patients and their families. The products range from books, organizations, cosmetics, cotton, and services (such as hot lines, toll-free numbers, and nonsmokers' services) to a wide variety of kosher and nonkosher food products (such as cereals, oils, spreads, sweeteners, and condiments). Updated periodically.

As You Live . . . And Breathe
New York, New York: American Lung Association, 1980
16 pages
Order from: your local American Lung Association affiliate
or
American Lung Association
1740 Broadway
New York, New York 10019
FREE, single copies

Through the use of brief, clear statements and excellent illustrations, students can learn about the process of breathing. The pamphlet describes the exchange of oxygen and carbon dioxide; how the respiratory system is affected by changes in climate; and the body's natural defenses against the assault of cigarette smoke, air pollution, dusts, and pathogens.

This excellent and attractive pamphlet often accompanies the showing of the film "Breathing Easy," also available through the American Lung Association (see page 96). It makes clear the working of the lungs and identifies their natural support system and enemies. The combination of the film and the pamphlet—or the pamphlet alone—can serve as the basis of classroom lessons for fourth grade through junior high school.

Asthma
Weinstein, Allan M., M.D.
New York, New York: McGraw-Hill Book Company, 1987
384 pages
Order from: publisher or you local bookstore
ISBN: 0–07–069058–8 Cloth $17.95

This is a thorough and comprehensive look at the problem of asthma for the person with asthma or the parents of a child with asthma. It provides the reader with a clear understanding of the nature of the illness and specific techniques to tailor a self-management plan, using a doctor's guidance to monitor and deal effectively with the condition. The book is divided into five sections: Understanding Asthma, Asthma Management, Asthma in Special Circumstances, Asthma Out of Control, and Special Problems. The asthma management or medication program section, which is the core of this book, offers highly specific information about asthma and its various treatments. At the close of each chapter is a brief summary, along with a number of questions that are frequently asked by patients and their families on the subject covered in the chapter. This format makes for an easy-to-read reference work.

Series of Pamphlets on Asthma and Allergies
Drug Allergy; Dust Allergy; Mold Allergy; Food Allergy; Insect
   Allergy; Pollen Allergy; Poison Allergy; Sinusitis
Bethesda, Maryland: National Institute of Allergy and Infectious
   Diseases, The National Institutes of Health
12 to 20 pages
Order from: Superintendent of Documents
U.S. Government Printing Office
Washington, D.C. 20402
or
The American Academy of Allergy and Immunology
6611 East Wells Street
Milwaukee, Wisconsin 53202
PRICE, Inquire

This is a series of highly informative pamphlets prepared by the Office of Research Reporting and Public Response of the National Institute of Allergy and Infectious Diseases. Each pamphlet succinctly discusses the symptoms, treatment, and prevention of the specific problem, including medications involved and new treatments available. There is even a brief comment or two on the new research being conducted on the respective allergy. Excellent reading.

Asthma and Hay Fever
Knight, Alan
New York, New York: Arco Publishing, Inc., 1981
123 pages
Order from: publisher or your local bookstore
ISBN: 0-668-04675-9 Cloth $11.95
ISBN: 0-668-04681-3 Paper $5.95

This book, available in hardcover and paperback editions, is well illustrated with clear diagrams and color photographs that explain how we breathe. Photographs also illustrate relaxation and breathing exercises. Clearly written and nontechnical, it is very useful for a lay audience.

Asthma Information
New York, New York: American Lung Association, 1982
16 pages
Order from: your local American Lung Association affiliate
or
American Lung Association
1740 Broadway
New York, New York 10019
FREE, single copies

This pamphlet deals with the special problems of asthma in children and is written for the nonmedical person in particular. It begins with an explanation of the body changes that occur in asthma and describes what constitutes childhood asthma, along with the psychological effects on the individual patient. The causes and the mechanisms that trigger asthma episodes are discussed, including an emphasis on how current medical therapy and the supportive role of the family and friends can help the child cope with the situation. The booklet points out how a patient can be guided to learn proper breathing and other exercises and take a limited part in sports. Readers also learn what is needed in the community at large in the way of supportive programs, as well as the role that lung associations can play in bringing such programs into being.

At the end of each section of text is a series of questions, which helps the reader determine whether he or she has understood the material. This form of self-testing also heightens the reader's sense of personal involvement. Recommended for parents and teachers of young children, especially parents of children with asthma.

Asthma Therapy: A Behavioral Health Care System for
  Respiratory Disorders
Creer, Thomas L.
New York, New York: Springer Publishing Company, 1979
Order from: publisher or your local bookstore
ISBN: 0-8261-2500-X Cloth $26.95

This book describes chronic obstructive lung diseases (COLD) and is divided into two major sections. The first defines COLD; discusses who is affected by it; and describes personality, psychological, and learning studies relating to asthma in children. The second part covers behavior and behavior modification. The book is technical but readable and ideal for someone who wants a comprehensive background book for asthma self-management programs.

Breathing Easy
The Asthmatic Children's Foundation of New York, Inc., 1985
17 pages
Order from: The Asthmatic Children's Foundation of New York,
  Inc.
Box 568
Spring Valley Road
Ossining, New York 10562
FREE, single copies

Part of a series the foundation has developed, this booklet focuses on breathing exercises and techniques to control asthma. In addition to the exercises, the booklet offers "Breathing Easy" games that teach effective breathing for individuals and groups. It also includes a score sheet. Very useful.

Breathing Exercises for Asthma
Butts, Karen R.
Springfield, Illinois: Charles C. Thomas, 1980
55 pages
Order from: publisher or your local bookstore
ISBN: 0-398-04104-0 Cloth $11.75

The book deals with breathing techniques and exercises designed to stimulate the body, relax muscles, and improve posture. It focuses on belly breathing, a technique that the author, who is a respiratory therapist, refers to as "complete" breathing. This book is recommended for parents of children with asthma, as well as health educators and physical education teachers.

Children with Asthma: A Manual for Parents
Plaut, Thomas, M.D.
Amherst, Massachusetts: Pedipress, 1984
156 pages
Order from: publisher or your local bookstore
ISBN: 0-914625-02-0 Paper $9.95

This is a superb book for parents of children with asthma. The author, a pediatrician who has specialized in the treatment of children with asthma, provides practical information that stresses self-care principles. One of the most appealing features of the book is its case histories, which illustrate the various problems and happy solutions many parents have discovered in living with children who have asthma. A reassuring book that combines medical information and personal involvement from a dedicated physician, it should dispel many of the fears and anxieties parents have concerning asthma.

Clearing the Air: A Guide to Quitting Smoking
Office of Cancer Communications, 1981
Order from: Office of Cancer Communications
Bldg 31, Room 10A18
National Institutes of Health
Bethesda, Maryland 20205
FREE, single copies

This pamphlet contains a variety of approaches that make the formidable task of quitting the smoking habit seem possible. The tips and helpful hints are illustrated by humorous line drawings. In addition to providing information on what happens after a person quits smoking, the pamphlet provides brief descriptions of formal programs for quitting and other sources of information. It addresses the fear of gaining weight and gives calorie counts for snack foods. It also has a good table of contents, which aids ease of comprehension, and each double-page spread contains one idea and one drawing so that the reader can absorb the material easily.

Dangers of Smoking, Benefits of Quitting,
  and Relative Risks of Reduced Exposure
New York, New York: American Cancer Society, 1980
81 pages
Order from: your local American Cancer Society unit
or
The American Cancer Society
777 Third Avenue
New York, New York 10017
FREE, single copy

This is a summary of the key scientific and medical studies on smoking plus new information on the economics, psychology, pharmacology, and other aspects of tobacco smoking and health. It's a new version of the book published by the American Cancer Society in 1972, adding to the earlier work by presenting the latest findings in the Surgeon General's report and the report "Controlling the Smoking Epidemic" of the World Health Organization. Although this book may alarm all but the most serious students of smoking, it is easy to understand and is fact-filled. Its lack of illustrations indicates that it is not intended to be light reading, although its reading level is high school.

Drug Information for the Consumer
United States Pharmacopeial Convention, 1987
1,202 pages
Order from: your local bookstore
or
Consumer Reports Books
Customer Service Center
P.O. Box 589
Stratford, Connecticut 06497–9984
paper $25.00

This is a compendium of information on nearly every prescription and over-the-counter drug currently marketed in the United States and Canada. Prepared by the United States Pharmacopeia (USP), which for more than 150 years has set the official national standards of strength, quality, purity, packaging, and labeling for drugs, the book has been designed exclusively to answer all the questions the general public may have concerning the use of all types of medications. Organized alphabetically by generic or family name, each entry covers the proper use and dosage of drugs; food, drinks, other medicines, and activities to be avoided while taking the drug; possible side effects of the drug; and precautions for pregnant women, nursing mothers, children, and the elderly. Handsome layout and easy to read.

Facts About Your Lungs
New York, New York: American Lung Association, 1974–1983
Leaflets
Order from: your local American Lung Association affiliate
or
American Lung Association
1740 Broadway
New York, New York 10019
FREE, single copies

This is a series of 22 leaflets covering a wide range of lung diseases and problems associated with the respiratory system. The subjects covered are asthma, bronchiectasis, chronic cough, cigarette smoking, cocci (coccidioidomycosis—a fungus disease of the lungs caused by inhaling plant spores), chronic bronchitis, the common cold, diseases caused by dust, emphysema, flu, hay fever, histo (histoplasmosis—a fungus-caused disease of the lungs), lung cancer, pipe and cigar smoking, pleurisy, pneumonia, sarcoidosis (a disease of the lungs), secondhand smoke, shortness of breath, and tuberculosis. Treatment as well as preventive measures are covered.

The entire series provides the reader with an easy-to-understand but global perspective of the respiratory system, problems associated with lung diseases, treatments for respiratory disorders, and measures to prevent lung disease.

Facts in Brief About Lung Disease
New York, New York: American Lung Association, 1981
15 pages
Order from: your local American Lung Association affiliate
or
American Lung Association
1740 Broadway
New York, New York 10019
FREE, single copies

This pamphlet is periodically updated to include information and facts about lung disease, including specific data on sickness and death and the economics of lung disease throughout the country. It also provides information on prevention and control, parents who smoke, colds and flu, pneumonia, bronchitis and emphysema, tuberculosis, asthma, fungus infections, and occupational lung disease. A final section is devoted to the American Lung Association, its many local affiliates throughout the country, and the variety of services they provide to the community.

Help Yourself to Better Breathing
Bowers, Margaret
New York, New York: American Lung Association, 1980
24 pages
Order from: your local American Lung Association affiliate
or

American Lung Association
1740 Broadway
New York, New York 10019
FREE, single copies

This pamphlet should have a strong appeal for those who are having breathing problems. It covers many of the problems most people face at some time in their lives. Starting with a basic, illustrated description of the lungs and their function, it takes up the common symptoms of coughing, sneezing, and shortness of breath. Proper methods of breathing are described, and simple exercises (illustrated by diagrams) are advised to clear the lungs of the mucus which has clogged the airways. The exercises shown have been found to help build a person's strength and enable the lungs to work more efficiently. One section deals with such common troublemakers as smoking, infections, and air pollution. The value of medicines and of various breathing aids as therapy are carefully considered, but in adopting any prescribed regimen the importance of following a doctor's orders is stressed. The final section covers proper diets and a well-balanced life-style as adjuncts in achieving and maintaining good health for everybody, especially those with lung problems.

The reading is made easy by its step-by-step format, and the text is set in large type. When giving direct advice, the book has a question-and-answer format that is compelling, and the illustrations are ample, clear, and easy to follow.

Home Care for the Chronically Ill or Disabled Child:
  A Manual and Sourcebook for Parents and Professionals
Jones, M.L.
New York: Harper & Row, 1985
321 pages
Order from: publisher or your local bookstore
Cloth $24.50, paperback $12.95

A practical guide to daily care of a chronically ill or disabled child, the book provides information on hospitalization, finding appropriate medical care, medication, respiratory therapy, bathing, toileting, dressing, and feeding. It also discusses play, recreation and travel, education, adolescence, organization of the home, and payments for medical treatment. It's illustrated, and appendices include a list of suggested readings.

Home Health Care: A Complete Guide
  for Patients and Their Families
Friedman, J.
New York: W.W. Norton, 1986
589 pages
Order from: publisher or your local bookstore
ISBN: 0–449–90230–7 Paper $14.95

This is a guide to information and resources related to home health care, but it is intended only to supplement your doctor's advice. Information is given on the benefits of home care; the home care system; health insurance; and preparation of the home, the patient, and the family. The book discusses daily living strategies, nutrition, medications, personal health care, pain, and home care technology. Among many health care problems, it specifically addresses respiratory disease.

How to Stop Smoking
South Deerfield, Massachusetts: Channing L. Bete Company, Inc.,
  1981
15 pages
Order from: publisher
FREE, single copy

This brief pamphlet opens with a review of the immediate and long-term ill effects of smoking on one's health, and cites the physical and psychological benefits of quitting. There are also short descriptions of the various methods currently in vogue for getting rid of the smoking habit, such as group or individual counseling, behavior modification, medical treatment, stop-smoking clinics, and hypnosis. Suggestions are offered for a do-it-yourself approach to quitting. Information is presented in a nonthreatening and nonmoralizing tone.

In Defense of the Lung
Green, Gareth M.
New York, New York: American Lung Association, 1974
16 pages
Order from: your local American Lung Asociation affiliate
or
American Lung Association
1740 Broadway
New York, New York 10019
FREE, single copies

This pamphlet concerns itself with the lung's defense mechanisms and how they are overcome by breathing in noxious and gaseous materials. After "Answers to Some Practical Questions," the concluding section, "What Can We Do," takes up practical methods for preventing respiratory disease, both in the individual and on a community-wide basis. In this latter context, several areas are covered: emergency services, intensive care, physical medicine, personal environmental control, and coordination of various efforts in a home care program.

The publication is informative and clearly written, giving the reader an understanding of what happens inside the lung when it is assaulted by foreign substances in the air. An outstanding feature in explaining the physical changes that take place in the lung is the use of photomicrographs taken by the scanning electron microscope. These illustrations, in which tissue sections are enlarged several thousand times and appear almost as three-dimensional images, show the nature of normal and diseased lung structure, down to the most minute cellular components. The reading level is high school and would be effective as a supplemental teaching aid for science students in high school or college, for persons going through an anti-smoking program, and for asthma patients.

Lungs Are for Life
New York, New York: American Lung Association, 1982–1983
Order from: your local American Lung Association affiliate
or
American Lung Association
1740 Broadway
New York, New York 10019
FREE, single copies

This is a series of four teaching guides for children from kindergarten through fourth grade. Each kit contains a teacher's guide, student activity sheets, action cards where appropriate, and posters. The purpose, as noted in the introduction, is to introduce children to health-related activities that will (1) lead them to an appreciation of their bodies and the importance of maintaining good lung health, (2) show them what contributes to lung health and what works against it, (3) help them to understand the alternatives open to them, and (4) challenge them to accept responsibility for making sound health choices.

The program focuses on five factors related to lung health: self-awareness, air quality and the environment, the respiratory system, health hazards, and commitment to a healthy lifestyle.

Lung Diseases of Adults
Luce, John, M.D.
New York, New York: American Lung Association, 1986
100 pages
Order from: your local American Lung Association affiliate
or
American Lung Association
1740 Broadway
New York, New York 10019
Price and availability may vary from affiliate to affiliate

The purpose of this book is to describe how the adult respiratory system works and how it is affected by common disorders, one of which is asthma. The first chapter outlines the structure and function of the respiratory system. The second introduces readers to the features of the patient history, physical findings, and laboratory tests that help doctors diagnose lung diseases. The remaining eight chapters divide these disorders primarily along anatomical lines. A definition of each disease is offered first, followed by its causes, its prevalence within the population, its effects upon the body, common symptoms, how the disease is diagnosed, and its treatment and prevention. Asthma is discussed as a disease of the lower airways. Although it is organized like a medical textbook, the book is written in an informal style and is suitable for the asthma patient who seeks an introduction to the larger picture of lung diseases. College reading level.

Lung Diseases of Children
Evans, Hugh, M.D.
New York, New York: American Lung Association, 1979
109 pages
Order from: your local American Lung Association affiliate
or
American Lung Association
1740 Broadway
New York, New York 10019
Price and availability may vary from affiliate to affiliate

In eight separate chapters the author presents in chronological order—from the newborn to the adolescent—the numerous types of lung disease in infants and children. The book covers the extent of the problem, lung diseases of the newborn, infections of early childhood, accidents of childhood, sudden infant death syndrome, chronic lung diseases of children, general diseases that cause pulmonary problems, and managing lung disease in children.

Despite the comprehensive scope of this publication, it is well organized and methodically arranged. The writing is clear and understandable for the nontechnical reader. College reading level.

Lung Hazards on the Job
New York, New York: American Lung Association, 1977–1983
Leaflet series
Order from: your local American Lung Association affiliate
or
American Lung Association
1740 Broadway
New York, New York 10019
FREE, single copies

The work environment contains many hazards, and minimizing and reducing these risks are important aspects of making your environment a healthy climate to work in. Each title examines a specific hazard to the lungs: Auto Repair (carbon monoxide, asbestosis, chromates, and solvents); Asbestos; Byssinosis (working with flax, hemp or cotton); Fire Fighting (carbon monoxide); Hypersensitivity Pneumonitis (farmer's lung); Irritant Gases (sulfur dioxide, chlorine, phosgene, ozone, nitrogen dioxide, and ammonia); Occupational Asthma; Silicosis (working in mining, foundries, tunneling, sandstone grinding, sandblasting, concrete breaking, granite carving, and china manufacturing); Solvents; and Welding (nitrogen dioxide, ozone, and fluorides). The materials are well written and presented in a style that is easy to follow and read.

Respiratory Disorders
South Deerfield, Massachusetts: Channing L. Bete Company, Inc., 1981
16 pages
Order from: your local American Lung Association affiliate
or

American Lung Association
1740 Broadway
New York, New York 10019
PRICE, Inquire

This is a series of illustrated pamphlets designed to make for a quick and easy assimilation of essential information and pertinent facts. The four titles are: "About Asthma," "About Lungs and Lung Diseases," "About Smoking and Cancer," and "On-the-Job Respiratory Protection." The asthma pamphlet, which may be of more interest to the readers of this book, features asthma information interwoven with line drawings. It begins with a description of asthma and cites reasons why this is such an important problem. It reviews the causes of asthma, describes how the lungs function during an asthma attack, and cites some of the predisposing factors which may lead to the illness. Various treatments are reviewed and suggestions provided for relieving asthma episodes and avoiding episodes of the illness. Highly readable.

Shortness of Breath (Third Edition)
Moser, Archibald, Hansen, Ellis, and Whelan
(Pulmonary and Critical Care Division
   University of California, San Diego)
St. Louis, Missouri: C.V. Mosby Company, 1983
105 pages
Order from: publisher
PRICE, Inquire

This book reflects some of the most up-to-date techniques for respiratory care. Its basic premise is that patients with shortness of breath can become active members of the treatment team, accepting (and enjoying) the fact that they must play a central role in their own care. Starting with a brief introduction to the function of the lungs and an equally brief discussion of the various medications and breathing paraphernalia, the book offers many handy and well-illustrated examples of breathing, coughing, and relaxation exercises. It also touches on matters such as diet, smoking, and what to do in an emergency. The 130 illustrations are very appealing.

Superstuff
New York, New York: American Lung Association, 1981
Packet
Order from: your local American Lung Association affiliate
or
American Lung Association
1740 Broadway
New York, New York 10019
PRICE, Inquire

This is a self-help packet of educational materials aimed for the more than two million children with asthma under seventeen years of age. It consists of a newsmagazine-formatted publication, an eighty-eight-page serial-bound book brimming with activities for children with asthma, an attractive poster, and a 33⅓ rpm record encouraging relaxation.

The newsmagazine offers information about asthma and answers questions raised by parents who have successfully coped with meeting the needs of a child with asthma. Also included are tips on how to recognize symptoms, helpful information on factors that trigger episodes of asthma, suggestions on exercise and nutrition, and explanations of medications used in controlling the illness.

Also in the packet is a child's activity book, printed on heavy paper, full of photos, illustrations, and diagrams related to activities and games which give the participant information about asthma and how to cope with it. Some of the specific topics covered include: (1) recognizing asthma signals, (2) becoming familiar with situations that trigger asthma, (3) learning how to relax with asthma, (4) learning how to cope with asthma, and (5) learning how to talk about asthma with others.

This is an excellent instructional packet for children with asthma as well as for parents, teachers, and those who work with them.

Tips to Remember Series
American Academy of Allergy and Immunology
14 (4-page) pamphlets
Order from: American Academy of Allergy and Immunology
611 East Well Street
Milwaukee, Wisconsin 53202
$0.25 each ($20.00 for first 100 copies; additional copies $10.00
    per 100 copies)

A series of colorful pamphlets containing educational information on asthma and allergies for the lay audience presented in a condensed, attractive, and readable format: #1) "Exercise-Induced Asthma and Bronchospasm"; #2) "Removing Dust and Other Allergic Irritants from Your Home"; #3) "Should You Get the 'Flu Shot'?"; #4) "Triggers of Asthma"; #5) "What Is an Allergic Reaction?" #6) "What's New in Allergy Research?" #7) "Allergic Contact Dermatitis"; #8) "Understanding the Pollen and Mold Season"; #9) "Occupational Asthma"; #10) "Hives"; #11) "Outpatient Treatment of Asthma"; #12) "What Every Patient Should Know About Asthma/Allergy Medications"; #13) "Adverse Reactions to Food Additives"; and #14) "Allergies to Animals."

What Do We Know About Allergies?
Irwin, Micheal, H.K.
New York, New York: Public Affairs Committee, 1978
28 pages
Order from: Public Affairs Pamphlets
381 Park Avenue South
New York, New York 10016
$0.50

This well-written pamphlet explains that allergy, or hypersensitivity, is a phenomenon which may account in part for many diseases in a wide segment of our population. After a brief historical overview, the author defines allergens and lists the four general classes of substances that bring about allergic reactions—inhalants, ingestants, contactants, and injectants. It offers an easy-to-understand look at mechanisms in the body—such as the production of antibodies—that bring about symptoms. The pamphlet fully describes the common forms of allergy: hay fever, asthma, dermatitis, hives, insect bites, food allergies, and medications. It also discusses several of the treatments for these factors, including desensitization for inhalant allergens and medications such as antihistamines and corticosteroids which provide at least temporary relief of symptoms. The role of the doctor in the diagnosis and treatment of any patient with an allergic condition is stressed.

Your Child's Lungs Are for Life
New York, New York: American Lung Association, 1980
14 pages
Order from: your local American Lung Association affiliate
or

American Lung Association
1740 Broadway
New York, New York 10019
FREE

This pamphlet is for parents. It presents useful information to help parents understand the respiratory needs of children and includes a discussion of specific ailments that can affect a child's lungs. It concludes with advice to pregnant women and information about lung distress in the newborn. Written in a clear and calm manner, it should be a welcome piece in a parent's library.

Audiovisual Materials

This section presents audiovisual materials recommended for patient use. The materials are listed in alphabetical order by title.

Should you be unable to find relevant audiovisual materials listed in the following pages, write to the American Lung Association for a list of the most recent films or tapes. Many public, professional, and medical libraries, including your local chapter of the American Lung Association, will have some of these materials available for rental. Check with the reference librarian at your local library to help you find the nearest source.

The Feminine Mistake
24 minutes, color, 16 mm and videocassette, 1978
Produced by Arnold Shapiro
Order from: Pyramid Film and Video
Box 1048
Santa Monica, California 90406
$425.00 (Purchase)
$55.00 (Rental)

The effects of cigarette smoking on a woman's body are demonstrated in a most graphic and impressive manner. We learn that cigarettes cause wrinkles, as well as more serious damage to the respiratory system and the heart and blood vessels. In one sequence, we see the telling effects of smoking on a fetus. At the close of the film, there is a harrowing interview with a woman dying of lung cancer. Although it borders on the sensational, the film presents a convincing, no-nonsense look at the harmful effects of smoking. This is a film for anyone—young or old—who remains unconvinced about the devastating effects of cigarette smoking.

How to Dust Proof Your Home
10 minutes, color, filmstrip and videocassette, 1980
Order from: Medfact
P.O. Box 418
Massillon, Ohio 44646
$145.00 (Purchase, filmstrip)
$160.00 (Purchase, videocassette)
No Rentals

Although allergens are found in most of our environments, we can control many of them. Substitutes for foods and products can be found that will reduce the number of allergy and asthma attacks. This film demonstrates one such strategy: lowering of the dust level in the home. The film offers some techniques for dustproofing the average home, which for many parents seems to be an impossible task initially. The pictures are attractive and clear, and the narrative easy to follow. The film offers positive reinforcement to the doctor's instructions for eliminating household allergens.

Introduction to Allergies
10 minutes, color, filmstrip and videocassette, 1981
Order from: Medfact
P.O. Box 418
Massillon, Ohio 44646
$145.00 (Purchase, filmstrip)
$160.00 (Purchase, videocassette)
No Rentals

As the title indicates, this program provides basic background information on allergies. Following a description of an allergy, there is an explanation of how various body systems are affected by common allergies. Various popular misconceptions are debunked. Although most of the information is carried by the narration on the sound track, the lively graphics and photographs show the effects of allergies on parts of the body and make the material easy to comprehend and highly useful.

Kids on the Block
Puppet kit
Order form: The Kids on the Block, Inc.
822 North Fairfax Street
Alexandria, Virginia 22314
PRICE, Inquire

This kit features a life-sized puppet named Scott Whitaker. Scott's a ten-year-old with asthma who has learned to cope with his condition. Through performances and dialogue with the audience, he helps children to understand what it's like to have asthma, allays many fears and misconceptions, and serves as a positive role model. The asthma puppet kit includes Scott, several scripts and dialogues, props, an asthma information resource list, and suggestions for educational follow-up activities about asthma.

Obstructive Lung Disease
16 minutes, 16 mm, videocassette and Super 8, 1979
Order from: Professional Research, Inc.
12960 Coral Tree Place
Los Angeles, California 90066
$295.00 (Purchase)
RENTAL, Inquire; also available in Spanish

In this film we follow a patient from examination through to treatment and aftercare. We learn a great deal about such diseases as emphysema, asthma, and chronic bronchitis. We also learn how the lungs work and how patients with lung illness can learn how to give themselves respiratory care through such techniques as breathing exercises. The many useful hints on how to cope with this kind of condition make this reassuring film particularly suited for the patient who is learning to live with a lung disease.

An Orientation to Asthma
Slide/audiocassette (ALA item #6140)
Order from: your local American Lung Association affiliate
or
American Lung Association
Department 190
1740 Broadway
New York, New York 10019

Price: Inquire through your local chapter as prices may vary from affiliate to affiliate (approximate price: $85.00)
No Rentals

The program is intended for health professionals and the general public. It reviews normal airway function and describes asthma episodes and their management.

An Orientation to the Lungs and Lung Disease
Developed and produced under the direction of the American Lung Association/American Thoracic Society Committee on Learning Resources
120 minutes, series of four 30-minute slides/audiocassettes, 1983
Order from: American Lung Association
Department 190
New York, New York 10019
$295.00 (Purchase complete series)
$85.00 (Purchase of individual programs)
No Rentals

The objective of this series is to provide a comprehensive introduction to the structure, function, and diseases of the human lungs. The series consists of four slide/cassette programs:

1. "An Orientation to the Structure and Function of the Lungs"—an overview of the anatomy of the chest, lungs, and heart; a discussion of the mechanics of breathing; and an explanation of how the respiratory system defends itself against inhaled hazardous substances and organisms.
2. "An Orientation to Chronic Obstructive Pulmonary Disease (COPD) and Lung Cancer"—a discussion of the two components of COPD (chronic bronchitis and emphysema) and a look at the progressive anatomical and functional changes in the lungs caused by chronic irritation, the irreversible damage caused by the long-term impact of COPD, and the nature of the uncontrolled growth of abnormal cells (lung cancer) arising from the airways.
3. "An Orientation to Asthma"—a review of the structure and function of normal airways, a description of the mechanisms responsible for asthma episodes and their symptoms and warning signs, a discussion of the diverse stimuli that trigger episodes and the diverse effects such episodes have on people's lives, and a presentation of

the management of the condition and the importance of positive attitudes of the family and friends of the asthma sufferer.

4. "An Orientation to Occupational and Infectious Lung Diseases"—a discussion of the lung diseases (pneumoconioses, hypersensitivity pneumonitis, viral and bacterial infections, and common fungal infections) caused by inhaled inorganic and organic dusts, toxic fumes and gases, and living organisms.

The program was designed for health care professionals and for patients with lung disease.

A Regular Kid
15 minutes, color, 16mm, 1981 (ALA item #6257)
Order from: your local American Lung Association affiliate
or
American Lung Association
Department 190
1740 Broadway
New York, New York 10019
Price: Inquire through your local chapter as prices may vary from affiliate to affiliate (approximate price: $188.00)
No Rentals

This film shows how children and their families cope with asthma problems. It is an upbeat look at the situation that parents and their children with asthma face. The film is especially designed and helpful for parents of children with asthma and school personnel.

Understanding Asthma
13 minutes, color, filmstrip and videocassette, 1980
Order from: Medfact
P.O. Box 418
Massillon, Ohio 44616
$145.00 (Purchase, filmstrip)
$160 (Purchase, videocassette)
No Rentals

This film provides an overview of what asthma is, what triggers attacks of bronchiospasm, and how people with asthma can learn to live with their condition. Diagrams show how mucus, swelling, and muscle spasms reduce the flow of air in the bronchial tubes. It positively and calmly stresses the fact that, although sensitivity is inherited, effective self-management of asthma requires the patient to understand more about the allergies that set off asthma episodes.

By means of animated diagrams, the nature of asthma and the role that allergies play in causing the disease are clearly demonstrated, with reference to the roles of allergens, respiratory infections, emotions, exercise, and aspirin. This is an excellent film for people with asthma and their families.

Who's in Charge Here?
14½ minutes, color, 16mm, 1979
Order from: your local American Cancer Society chapter
or
The American Cancer Society
777 Third Avenue
New York, New York 10017
FREE, loan

In a high school lab setting, students measure the immediate effects of smoking on their body processes. They measure temperature and pulse rates and the amount of carbon monoxide in their lungs before and after smoking a cigarette. A tremor test is used to illustrate the effects of smoking on the nervous system. In candid interviews, young people talk about how, when, where, and why they started smoking, and myths about the effects of smoking are confronted by facts. The film reinforces that physical damage begins with the first puff. By means of color animation, viewers are shown the effect of smoking on cilia and cells of the lungs, the spread of lung cancer, and the narrowing of heart vessels. The effects of smoking during pregnancy are explored, and a scientific test is shown which displays the effects of smoking on the blood vessels and heart. This interesting and fast-moving film is designed for teenagers, as well as parents and teachers of teenagers.

Women and Smoking
14 minutes, color, 16mm, 1981
Order from: your local American Cancer Society chapter
or
The American Cancer Society
777 Third Avenue
New York, New York 10017
FREE, loan

This film focuses on three women who are trying to cope with their smoking dilemma: a computer programer who smoked initially to relieve tension and to celebrate, a fundraiser who first smoked to appear sophisticated, and a housewife who started smoking because she thought it would make her look glamorous. For various reasons, all three women have now quit, and the story of the difficulties they had in quitting—as well as the rewards—comprise the heart of the film. This is not a preachy film. Rather, it's helpful and reassuring as it shows candid conversation with three likable people about how they successfully quit smoking. The music is catchy and perfectly matches the film's upbeat tone.

Your Doctor Talks to You About Asthma and Hay Fever
30 minutes, audiocassette, 1980
Order from: Soundwords
56-11 217th Street
Bayside, New York 11364
$10.95 (Purchase, audiocassette)
No Rentals

Two authorities on allergies, Stanley R. Fine, M.D., and Bernard R. Feldman, M.D., present information about asthma and hay fever. After defining the conditions and relating them to allergic diseases, they go on to cover the role of hereditary factors, asthma and emphysema, pollen, climate, foods, smoking, pets, emotions, immunotherapy, skin tests, treatment, and new research into prevention. Even though there is a great deal of information here for the person who may be concerned about only one form of allergy or allergy-related problem—asthma—the tape's comprehensiveness will be helpful for that person to achieve a clearer picture of the whole spectrum of allergic reactions. The authors are adept at explaining all of the technical terms in the film.

INDEX

"Useful, illuminating, even life-saving information."
Los Angeles Times

WOMANCARE:
A GYNECOLOGICAL GUIDE TO YOUR BODY
Lynda Madaras and
Jane Patterson, M.D., F.A.C.O.G.
with Peter Schick, M.D., F.A.C.S.

Written with a deep and compassionate understanding of women's special physical and emotional needs, this encyclopedic work goes further than any other book to give you a full range of information, treatments and alternatives— to allow you to choose the one with which you are most comfortable, and enable you to share more fully with your doctor the responsibility and care of your own health. It contains the most up-to-date material on the break-throughs in technique and research that are revolutionizing women's health care and treatment almost daily.

960 pages and over 100 charts and drawings give you detailed information on self-examination, menstruation and meno-pause, birth controls—safety, effectiveness and long-term effects of all options—doctor-patient relationships, DES and fertility drugs, and much, much more. A 500-page section on diseases covers everything from minor infections to cancer.

"Invaluable...Well organized, complete and easy to understand ...The most comprehensive gynecology text published to date."
Library Journal

"Impressive...WOMANCARE is a full-scale reference work. ...Women thus informed will know and like themselves better, recognize bad medical care and have the ammunition to stand up to their doctors when necessary." *Savvy*

AVON Trade Paperback 87643-4/$12.95 US/ $14.95 Can

Buy these books at your local bookstore or use this coupon for ordering:
....
Avon Books, Dept BP, Box 767, Rte 2, Dresden, TN 38225
Please send me the book(s) I have checked above. I am enclosing $_____
(please add $1.00 to cover postage and handling for each book ordered to a maximum of three dollars). *Send check or money order*—no cash or C.O.D.'s please. Prices and num-bers are subject to change without notice. Please allow six to eight weeks for delivery.

Name _____

Address _____

City _____ State/Zip _____

Womancare 1/87

THE GROUNDBREAKING #1
NEW YORK TIMES BESTSELLER BY
ADELE FABER & ELAINE MAZLISH

"Have I got a book for you!...
Run, don't walk, to your nearest bookstore."*Ann Landers*

SIBLINGS WITHOUT RIVALRY
How to Help Your Children Live Together
So You Can Live Too
70527-3/$7.95 US/$9.95 Can

don't miss their landmark book
HOW TO TALK SO KIDS WILL LISTEN
AND LISTEN SO KIDS WILL TALK
57000-9/$6.95 US/$8.95 Can

"Will get more cooperation from children than all the
yelling and pleading in the world."
Christian Science Monitor

and also
LIBERATED PARENTS, LIBERATED CHILDREN
00466-6/$3.95 US/$4.95 Can

Buy these books at your local bookstore or use this coupon for ordering:

Avon Books, Dept BP, Box 767, Rte 2, Dresden, TN 38225

Please send me the book(s) I have checked above. I am enclosing $_____
(please add $1.00 to cover postage and handling for each book ordered to a maximum of
three dollars). Send check or money order—no cash or C.O.D.'s please. Prices and numbers are subject to change without notice. Please allow six to eight weeks for delivery.

Name _____

Address _____

City _____ **State/Zip** _____

Faber&Mazlish 5/88

THE COMPLETE GUIDE TO A LIFETIME OF WELL-BEING BY AMERICA'S MOST TRUSTED HEALTH WRITER

JANE BRODY'S
The New York Times
— GUIDE TO —
PERSONAL HEALTH

Illustrated with graphs and charts, fully indexed and conveniently arranged under fifteen sections:

NUTRITION	SEXUALITY AND
EMOTIONAL HEALTH	REPRODUCTION
ABUSED SUBSTANCES	DENTAL HEALTH
EYES, EARS, NOSE AND	ENVIRONMENTAL HEALTH
THROAT	EFFECTS
SAFETY	SYMPTOMS
PESKY HEALTH PROBLEMS	COMMON SERIOUS
COMMON KILLERS	ILLNESSES
EXERCISE	MEDICAL CARE

COPING WITH HEALTH PROBLEMS

"Jane Brody's encyclopedia of wellness covers everything."
Washington Post

64121-6/$12.95 US/$16.95 Can

Buy these books at your local bookstore or use this coupon for ordering:

Avon Books, Dept BP, Box 767, Rte 2, Dresden, TN 38225
Please send me the book(s) I have checked above. I am enclosing $_____
(please add $1.00 to cover postage and handling for each book ordered to a maximum of
three dollars). *Send check or money order*—no cash or C.O.D.'s please. Prices and numbers are subject to change without notice. Please allow six to eight weeks for delivery.

Name _____

Address _____

City _____ State/Zip _____

JB-1/87